The events and conversations in this book have been written to the best of the author's ability, although some names and details have been changed or left vague to protect the privacy of individuals including the author and his most beloved fishing spots. Please be reminded that this has been written by a fisherman and the truth can be *gestures hands in an expanding motion* variable over time.

Always check your local laws and regulations regarding angling and angler access and seek the landowner's permission if it is needed. If you happen to come across a stream from references in this book, please be respectful, leave no trace, and refrain from posting locations on social media platforms.

Copyright © 2025 by Ben Michael Hohnke.

All rights reserved. No part of this book may be reproduced or used in any manner without written permission of the copyright owner, except for the use of quotations within book reviews.

First edition November 2025

Cover design by Sarah Hohnke

ISBN 978-1-7643870-0-2

ISBN 978-1-7643870-1-9 (ebook)

Published by Hohnke Outdoors

www.hohnkeoutdoors.com

Rivers of Passage

Adolescence to Fatherhood on Trout Streams

Ben Hohnke

Hohnke Outdoors

For my children. I pray you find your place in life much easier than I did.

Contents

Preface	1
Chapter 1 – Exploration	3
Chapter 2 – The Guy Fawkes River	11
Chapter 3 – Stream Hopping	21
Chapter 4 – Close To Home	31
Chapter 5 – On My Own	38
Chapter 6 – Cracking the Code	45
Chapter 7 – Full Submersion	49
Chapter 8 – Delayed Drying	59
Chapter 9 – The Little Styx	63
Chapter 10 – The Styx	72
Chapter 11 – Along Came Sarah	81
Chapter 12 – Within an Hour	91
Chapter 13 – The Trout Farm	99
Chapter 14 – Into The Trees	105

Chapter 15 – Dorrigo Gentlemens Gathering	110
Chapter 16 – Trifecta	121
Chapter 17 – Life is Fine Between the Pines	129
Chapter 18 – Sheba Shenanigans	137
Chapter 19 – Fireflies	147
Chapter 20 – New Parents	157
Chapter 21 – Three Weekends, Three Species	167
Chapter 22 – The World Changed	183
Chapter 23 – Embers	189
Chapter 24 – Rebuilding What Was Lost	197
Chapter 25 – Snow Flake Caddis	203
Chapter 26 – Life is Fine Even Without the Pines	218
Chapter 27 – One For James	228
Acknowledgments	242
References	245

Preface

Humanity has a long history of rituals, journeys, and milestones that we ultimately like to refer to as rites of passage. Events that signify a boy's journey into manhood, or a girl's journey into womanhood. In modern western civilisation, this has mostly been lost.

As a teenager, I found myself mostly adrift in life's current, coasting through school and life, hoping that if I shut my eyes to the pain I would eventually be carried downstream somewhere different.

Now almost two decades later, with a son of my own, I began to reflect on my life and determine at what point I actually made that passage from an adolescent crashing downstream with his eyes shut, to a man leading his family through life.

What I realised was that my rite of passage could not be traced to a single ritual or milestone, but rather a series of adventures – misadventures really, that mostly occurred by a trout stream with a rod in hand. So I decided to start writing parts of this wild journey down into a book.

This isn't a technical book on fishing for trout in the New England region of New South Wales, although I'm sure you may learn a thing or two from the contents. This is a story about a life lived alongside and shaped by the rivers of this area.

The pages I have written follow the rivers that carried me from my adolescent curiosity to a lifestyle I am now beginning to share with my own children.

Someone almost loses a finger, someone else falls off a ledge into jagged rocks, cars get stuck or spin out of control, rules are bent and ignorantly broken, love is found, children are born, there are droughts, fires, floods, feasts, and of course trout. All are intertwined on the following pages.

So if you are just after fly patterns, techniques, and locations – buy this book and skim read it anyways before you pass it on to a friend.

Chapter 1 – Exploration

January 2009

I found myself in a strange period of life. Caught between graduating high school, finding a job and starting work. Some people in my graduating year already had jobs before graduation and others were heading off to the universities in the cities. Some girls were about to have babies with questionably older men.

I didn't have a clue what I wanted to do in life. My only goal was to find a job that paid well and to go hunting and fishing as often as possible – two things that seemed to anchor me within the raging currents of my life. But I hadn't found a job yet. I was staying with my grandparents on the outskirts of Tamworth NSW, had applied for half a dozen jobs, but heard absolutely nothing.

One afternoon a few weeks into summer, I was out in the yard practicing my fly casting. I'd caught a carp a few years earlier in Quirindi Creek, as well as one unlucky rainbow trout after a half-day casting tuition near Launceston Tasmania, so I was keen to improve my skills. Then my phone started ringing, I was hoping it was someone offering me a job interview. But the caller ID showed that it was my best mate from school, Jason.

Jason and I were born on the same day in the same hospital, though never met until high school. I got Jason involved in archery and bowhunting. But lately we had been more interested in chasing fish in nice cool water rather than hiking mountains in the harsh Australian summer.

"What are you doing?" asked Jason.

"Nothing really, practicing my fly casting and waiting by the phone for job offers."

"Remember those streams I drove over near Ebor I said looked very 'trouty', want to go see if they are?"

I hesitated for a moment before agreeing to go on the recon mission. "Sure. When?"

"I'll be in Tamworth in an hour, grab your gear and something to sleep in."

So I packed my fly rod away – as I still wasn't ready to leave my comfort zone of spin fishing, at which I was very proficient – and got ready.

It was just after lunchtime when Jason pulled into the drive in his Mitsubishi Magna, with a crooked red 'P' sign hanging off the number plate. We shared the usual small talk while I packed my gear in: one rod, a box of trout lures, a drink bottle, snacks, a sleeping bag and an alleged four-man tent.

CHAPTER 1 – EXPLORATION

Jason suggested we go to the tackle shop first and grab a couple of extra lures just in case, so we did.

The old shop owner was a kind but weathered old bloke, who showed us some new minnow lures in trout colours that looked pretty good, and cheaper than the usual classic hard bodies. We bought a couple each.

"Where are you headed?" he asked.

"Up to Ebor, we haven't fished there before but hoping to find some trout."

"I know a good a spot – because you are young and fit, drive to the lower lookout below the second falls. Walk down the steep hill and you will find heaps of trout."

We thanked him and he wished us luck.

But then, in the car and heading north along the New England Highway, Jason and I discussed how freely he'd given us the spot. If it was any good, why would he tell us? If he knew, then everyone surely knew and it would be overfished. We debated a hundred different scenarios and questioned the advice with a healthy amount of scepticism.

Like most 17-year-olds do, we pulled into a fast-food restaurant en route for a leg stretch, to grab some snacks and cool drinks – even driving, it was hot and Armidale sits 980m above sea level. Then, with a couple of cheap burgers and some frozen drinks, we got back in the car and headed east on the waterfall way.

A mix of grazing country, national parks and a few creek crossings seemed to fly past in a blur in the early afternoon light. The vegetation changed to large eucalypt trees and banksias that crept closer and closer to the road edge, giving the appearance of a parted sea of bushland.

Finally, we approached the T-intersection and made the right turn. The next sign informed us that Ebor was only 3km away. My excitement was building a little bit by now, and I had been periodically checking the glass window with the back of my hand to monitor the outside temperature. It had been getting progressively cooler since we left Armidale. Perfect.

Following signs from the highway, it was only a short drive to the lower lookout suggested by the tackle shop owner. There were then two sets of falls, with the top falls being the most photographed and visited. I have no idea why since as we were to discover the lower falls are much larger and awe inspiring.

The Guy Fawkes River itself was named so because Major Edward Parke, a British colonist, happened to camp nearby on Guy Fawkes Day in 1845. The history of the site of course stretches back long before British colonisation, with archaeological evidence suggesting that the river served as a trade passage for the Gumbaynggirr people between the coast and the northern tablelands, and had been inhabited for roughly 10,000 years.

While I'm not of Aboriginal descent I have to agree that, when they picked the name 'Martiam', which means 'Great Falls' in native tongue (NSW National Parks), it was a far more deliberate and compelling name than a British colonist naming it after a co-conspirator of a gunpowder plot attempting to blow up British

CHAPTER 1 – EXPLORATION

parliament along with the king and his family in 1605 (Britannica).

In any event, the landscape from the falls downstream through the Guy Fawkes River National Park seemed largely unaffected by British colonisation. Towering eucalypts reached from the valley floor, outstretching to the sky with their pale white trunks and sage green foliage both striking and dull, stunning in a uniquely Australian way. Large chunky boulders the size of cars lay scattered across the valley like ruins of a collapsed building long abandoned and covered over in new green growth.

From there all we could see was water cascading over, before crescendoing into a large pool of brown-green water below. The impact of the falls generates its own misting system and the fern life appeared to be flourishing in a perfect circle around its base, and even on the cliffs behind the sheet of water itself.

Jason and I stood there at the lookout platform without speaking a word for a good period of time. Then we both look around, simultaneously thinking 'how the hell do we get down'. From where we stood looking toward the falls, there were only sheer vertical rocks. And back behind us, while it wasn't a rock face, the sloping hillside was still almost vertical.

"I'm not sure about this, hey." Jason huffed. "Do you think he was just having a lend of us?"

"He seemed pretty confident. Maybe he meant that small strip of river between the two falls?" I added.

"No, he seemed to emphasise the lower falls," Jason replied.

I had done some work at a rainbow trout farm the previous year, and remember my boss telling me that trout are coated in a slime that protects them while they go up and down rivers and across rocks. But I doubted that a fish would survive not just one, but two sets of falls, to even end up below the lower falls. "We could bust ourselves getting down there for nothing. He's probably laughing his ass off thinking of us standing here right now."

Jason made the call – it looked steep but really it wasn't 'that far' to the river.

I reluctantly agreed and we rigged up our rods. I had a one piece – a seven-foot 1-3kg rod with a 4lb braid – and Jason had a small Strudwick rod that was essentially the perfect small creek trout rod. The year before he had found it in the clearance rack of a snowy mountains tackle shop, on our way to a June long weekend snowboarding and fishing trip at Jindabyne and Perisher. So we got them ready. I tied on a favourite classic hardbody in rainbow trout colours and Jason tied on a trusty spinner. We packed some drink bottles into our repurposed school bags, along with our tackle boxes and some spools of spare leader material. Then it was a case of one last glance over the edge and into the abyss!

Cautiously beginning our descent, already feeling the pain of the walk back out, we eased ourselves down.

Now, the Australian bush is not something that I would call peaceful or relaxing. Some people might be offended by this, but I think if you took the sounds of the bush and its birdlife and recorded it for a meditation CD it would not help you achieve the desired result of relaxation and ambient background you desired. Black cockatoos screech at pitches that could rupture eardrums, while you listen to the mocking laugh of kookaburras mocking your fishing skills, or lack thereof. This is of course assuming you can hear anything over the constant noise of cicadas.

Here, though, the clashing of the water created a persistent rumble of sound that we not only heard, but felt across our bodies, not just from the big falls but from the series of boulder drops in the gorge below. So, no, these were not sounds that induced feelings of relaxation and overwhelming calm; these were sounds that incited adventure with an undercurrent that whispered 'caution'.

In terrain such as this, caution is a good thing – one wrong move on the descent and you would be hard-pressed trying to stop your fall. Your best options would be to hit a gum tree or try and latch onto a clump of the endemic razor grass that carpeted that side of the valley. It was also snake season at that time of year, and the area was home to a handful of the world's most venomous snakes, including tiger snakes.

After climbing amongst the loose rock and razor grass using our hands and feet, we switched tactics and got on our backsides and began a careful slide through the loose rock. At this stage we had descended a fair way and thought the river was close. We could really hear it.

But as we made our way through some fallen timber and loose rocks on a flat, we realised we had only reached a bench on the hillside about halfway down.

The next section wasn't as steep but it was full of large fallen trees, scrubby bushes and uneven rocks. The perfect scenario to break your ankle and have to get winched out by the rescue helicopter.

The question was: should we continue.

Chapter 2 – The Guy Fawkes River

Fate and gravity answered for us, and pulled us towards the river.

We broke through some chest high shrubs and got our first close-up look of the river. Upstream we could see the white blanket of water coming from the lower falls. The river was on average about twelve feet across and its banks down here were made of nothing but lichen and moss-covered rock. The water was a murky brown, grey and green hybrid – you could not see the bottom except in very shallow pockets between rocks. When I crouched down and put my hand in the water, it was ice cold.

Our usual tactic was to walk downstream and fish upstream so as to not spook the trout by approaching them front-on while they are facing into the current. That wouldn't be necessary here with all the pools essentially separated by their own mini waterfalls, combined with the murky water and boulders lining the edges. There was plenty of cover for us.

I walked to the pool slightly upstream of where we had emerged and Jason took the pool below. The pool was only about twenty feet long and had a small dog-leg shape to it. A small bubble line coming down indicated the main current, with no way of telling how deep it was at all. I felt a rising scepticism of the existence of any trout here, but it was soon drowned out by my surroundings and youthful optimism.

I flipped the bail arm on my little reel and pitched a cast to the head of the pool where a small waterfall came into it. Then I flipped the bail arm back and began a steady retrieve with an occasional twitch worked into it. I worked the lure right up to my feet.

Nothing.

The doubts came creeping back, but I made the second cast. The lure was almost back at my feet when I saw a silver flash behind it, as the water ever so gently boiled where the flash had been.

I was excited now, my heart racing. I turned downstream to convey the message to Jason when I saw his little rod load up. "Yep! I'm on!" I quickly rock-hopped my way down and netted the fish for him, just as we had learnt years ago to work together to land fish.

In the net before us was a perfect rainbow trout. She was a sleek silver, with a gentle blush pink stripe and a generous coating of freckles coating the back to the lateral line. We took a few pictures and released the fish back into the river, shared a high five and made our way upstream. Jason proceeded to catch a couple more near identical sized rainbow trout, while I struggled with zero interest in my lure.

CHAPTER 2 – THE GUY FAWKES RIVER

Later, we scrambled across the slipperiest rocks I have ever experienced in search of other pools, in what can only be described as a minefield of the worst-shaped and sized rocks, never knowing which one was going to roll away when you stood on it and which one your foot would slip off anyway. The reason they were so slippery was because we were almost at the base of the giant waterfall now.

We had entered a microecosystem. The air was filled with mist, ferns poked out of any small pocket of dirt caught in the rock cavities, and the surrounding vegetation in the radius of the falls was noticeably greener. Clearly benefiting from their close proximity.

This was the biggest pool. You couldn't cast all the way to the top of the pool from the tail. If there was going to be a monster fish it would be in here. We worked that hole over for more than an hour, for nothing more than a few tiny bumps. A small hatch of something started and trout the size of a finger began launching out of the water to intercept their prey. We observed for a while to see if anything bigger surfaced, but nothing did.

Maybe the giant waterfall was annoying to senior trout? Maybe the big ones were wiser toward lure offerings? All I knew is that I was getting a headache from the rumble of the falls. So we made our way back across the slippery rock minefield, and back past where we first emerged onto the river to the pools below.

The roar of the water was more of background noise here and my head felt clearer. Jason brought another couple of fish to hand,

and with no more interest in my lure I cut it off and tied on a copper and black spinner.

I jumped down a few big rocks to position myself at the tail end of the pool. The mid-afternoon sun was starting to get the ominous glow that announced it probably wasn't as early in the day as we thought. But I still hadn't caught a fish and Jason had landed a healthy half dozen.

The pressure was building. I made a nice cast. The thing I love about spinners is that it is unmistakable to know if the lure is swimming correctly, you give them a few winds and they crank over like gears. You can feel this as a steady humming baseline through your rod. The second that stops, you know you have either hit weed or another snag, or you're about to hook a fish.

Thankfully, when that hum stopped, I felt my rod dip down and a fighting fit trout pulled enthusiastically on the line. I was always nervous fighting fish, only relaxing once I saw the net come out of the water with the fish still in it. With this particular trout, I already knew it was the fish of the day – forty plus centimetres of silver New England trout goodness. "Quality over quantity," I sarcastically said to Jason. Not that it was a competition. Still, we always light-heartedly ragged each other out.

The light was fading now, though, so once I'd landed the fish and set it free again, satisfied that I wasn't leaving with a doughnut, we began the scramble back up the hill.

We always knew deep down that this walk out would be hell, but the elation from finding those trout had dumbed down our senses. Just like a bucket of ice dropped over your head, the elation had fled and the dread of the climb remained.

We made it to the first bench relatively easily, but then were met with the sheer vertical nature of the next part of the slope. Climbing on our hands and knees, traversing across the face diagonally, we had to grab purchase on any grass clumps that we could find. A few times entire clumps ripped right out of the shallow rocky ground and almost sent us rolling back down the hill. In other barren patches, we had no choice but to grab a hold of thin-rooted razor grass as a safety hold.

We were only about halfway up when we had both had enough. "Next time, we bring abseiling gear," I said jokingly – knowing deep down it was a good idea, just not financially viable.

We could now see the lookout platform – it was directly above us with a small family on the deck. The father leant over the edge and looked at Jason and I before turning around and ushering his family away. I must admit it must have been a sight to see: two people come crawling up the slope below you on their hands and knees.

When we finally crested that top lip of the slope, I lay flat on the ground. A euphoric feeling of accomplishment swept over me. You could have told me I just summited Everest or K2, I wouldn't have cared. It couldn't possibly be better than how I felt at that moment.

Like most teenage boys, we had worked up quite the appetite. We drove into the town of Ebor. On the left, sitting on the banks of the Guy Fawkes River, was the local pub; on the right was a small cafe in a very old cottage, which had been closed for some time.

Nothing much beats a counter meal at a pub in Australia for price and portion size. So we pulled into the pub, not that we had any other options. We ordered a couple of cold soft drinks, as we weren't quite eighteen, then scanned the room. Pictures of people with big trout scattered the walls, mostly faded and cracked to time. Two roughly four-to-five pound taxidermy rainbow trout hung proudly above the bar on their wooden boards, decades old.

The publican was a nice middle-aged bloke with dark hair, probably glad to see some new faces. The other patrons were either locals or had been made to feel like locals by how freely they talked with the publican.

"Are you boys chasing a feed?" asked the publican.

We nodded and ordered the chicken schnitzel that was on the special board. The meals didn't take long and, in true country style, they came out on large white plates. The schnitzel was about an inch thick and took up over half the plate, the other half was filled with the usual chips and salad.

"What type of steroids has this chicken been on?" I said in jest.

We had a good chuckle and, for lack of a better word, demolished the meal.

When clearing the plates afterwards, the publican asked us what we had been up to and where we were staying.

"Just been fishing today," I said. "Haven't decided where to stay yet. Bought some camping gear, but wondering if you had any accommodation?"

"Sorry, boys," the publican replied, "I'm all booked up tonight, but if we get some bad weather or you're stuck you can roll a swag out under the verandah section at the front."

There is a certain quality that rural business owners have and I think it's the ability to let you down but lend you a hand at the same time. While you feel a little bit dejected (not that our lack of planning was his fault), you still hold them in esteem enough to never say a bad word about their business, and are more likely to stop in there again in future.

We thanked him for the meal and the offer, paid our bill and walked back out the front door to the car. The sun was just beginning to set and a middle-aged woman with bleached blonde hair was swatting flies while she finished a cigarette. The sky had turned grey and a pink band – not unlike those on the trout we had caught that day – circled the horizon. It had been a great day.

We drove back down to the lookout and the sun was set now. We parked the car next to a series of knee-high timber bollards designed to stop anyone from driving into the picnic area. The bollards must have been a fair age as there was lichen growing from them.

We popped the boot of the car, grabbed the little tent and an old dolphin torch, and got to work on pitching it.

The stars were out now and there was no one around. We spread our sleeping bags out in the four-man two-actual-human-beings tent and tried to get to sleep.

Jason was asleep within five mins, as his steady breathing turned into a light snore.

His light snore got louder, though, until I pushed him a little and he rolled over and was quiet. Then I realised that the snoring was the least of my worries, as there in the background was the constant crashing of the water over the falls.

I don't remember falling asleep, but I do know I woke up a few hours later to the moon coming down on the tent and illuminating its navy and beige panels. I rolled onto my belly to escape the brightness, but couldn't commit to sleep with the sound of the falls. I don't really know how much I slept. I just know I was awake for a lot of the night.

Later, I woke again, though this time I could tell by the laugh of kookaburras and calls of the magpies that dawn was approaching.

Jason was still fast asleep. I envied how well he could sleep, but climbed out of the tent still in my clothes from the day before, found my shoes and went to the pit toilets. I walked over the lookout platform thinking, if this behemoth is going to keep me awake most of the night, I may as well appreciate it.

I sat for a while on top of a picnic table with my feet on the seat, watching the sun rise above the gums in the east. I took in the fresh mountain air and the bird life. It was single-digit temperatures, though, and a bit cold. So I grabbed the keys out of the tent, popped the boot and grabbed the hoody that I had reluctantly taken on Grannie's advice.

"It gets cold up there," she had said. "Take a jumper or you will catch a chill."

I think Pa saw that I didn't believe her, so added, "trust me, you'll need it."

So I packed it. I don't know why we are so stubborn as teenagers to people who are older, especially ones that genuinely care for us.

Anyway, I changed my shirt, zipped up my hoody, and shut the boot. As I turned away from the car, I saw a sign that made my stomach drop:

Day use only. Camping prohibited.

Oh crap.

I quickly went back to the tent, woke Jason up and told him about the sign. He jumped out and we quickly packed down the tent, rolled up our sleeping bags and threw them in the boot. Phew! The rangers could have driven by at any minute and fined us. Now there was no evidence we'd stayed overnight.

Then Jason said he was hungry and pulled out a small watermelon, which Pa had grown and given us to take.

"Have you got a knife?" I asked Jason.

He nodded, grabbed one of his hunting knives out of the car, then got to work slicing it up. About halfway through a cut, he shrieked out, threw down the knife and jumped up from the table. He was pacing around and holding the end of his left pinky.

A trail of blood followed where he was pacing. Of course he'd cut himself!

I grabbed the first aid kit out of the car, and got Jason to sit down. He took his right hand off his pinky and... he had completely sliced off the outer side of his pinky from knuckle to nail! Naturally it was bleeding bad. So I gave him some dressings and we bandaged his hand up.

It was *just* enough. The blood was soaking through a little bit, though not enough to redo the dressing.

"It looks like you cut off that section of your finger," I told him. "I don't know how that's going to look when it grows back."

He picked up the knife and there was a section of the side of his pinky about an inch long perched on the edge of the blade. "Oooo, that is nasty!" he said.

"You're not wrong!" I replied.

Jason flicked his chunk of flesh off the blade and onto the ground. A piece of him would live there forever now.

I cleaned down the blade with an alcohol swab from the first aid kit, then carefully finished slicing the melon. We sat on top of the picnic table, feet on the seats, looking out at the falls and ate the melon in the morning light.

Chapter 3 – Stream Hopping

"How's your finger?" I asked Jason after our breakfast.

"Yeah, alright. It's just throbbing like mad," he replied. He took a couple of paracetamol and we climbed into the car. "Where shall we fish now? I'm not going down that hill again," said Jason.

"I concur!" I replied.

"How about... When I was driving to Iluka for our schoolies fishing trip, I drove over some awesome-looking streams. They looked super trouty," said Jason.

"Only one way to find out!"

So we turned back onto the main road and drove through Ebor. The sun was just coming over the ridges of the weatherboard cottages, and the grass on the verges was heavy with dew. There only appeared to be a single row of cottages dotting the highway before we passed a service station, then the town was gone.

It wasn't long before we passed a nice-looking stream. It weaved its way up through a shallow valley with barely any trees along its edges, was flowing well and had dark clear water flowing through it. We slowed down and pulled over. The shoulder of the road wasn't particularly wide and you couldn't really safely park a car here. There was also a big sign on a fence that crossed the stream:

Private Property, Trespassers Will Be Prosecuted.

"I guess that rules this one out," I said to Jason.

So we drove a little further along and found a dirt road turning off the main road. Hoping to find a better access spot for the creek, we took the turning. But after fifteen minutes of driving and getting no closer to the stream, we turned back around and came back onto the highway.

Soon, we approached a T-intersection and turned right, following a sign to Dorrigo.

Around a sweeping bend, we descended into a large open valley, laden with fog. There was another stream at the bottom with a nice area to pull over. We parked the car next to a white sedan already parked under a tree. We got our rods and bags and walked to the water.

The creek was about eight to ten feet across and flowing well. The water was clear but looked dark due to the rocks beneath. The banks were lined with grass and tussock. Slightly upstream, a fly fisherman was walking back towards us. With his rod in one hand, he lifted up the tip of the rod and caught the fly in that hand, then hooked it onto the rod's hook keeper, and wound the reel until the belly of the beige fly line came up tight against the rod.

"Any luck?" I asked as he got closer.

"Nah, nothing," he replied. "The water looks perfect, but you can only really fish about 50m up, then you hit a fence. I think it gets flogged here pretty hard." So he wished us luck, packed his rod in the car and drove off.

We made our way upstream to see if the fish would like our offerings better than his fly.

Not even a non-committal trout followed the lure in.

We got to the fence, it was pretty old and so full of holes that you could walk right through it. In New South Wales at that time (and as of writing), there is a law that allows you to fish in a river or creek providing you access it legally, i.e. not by walking across a farmer's field to get to it. It's okay if you can access it from a bridge or public access point, but you can't go above the top of the bank, as you'd be technically trespassing at that point.

Still, we walked through the fence, sticking to the bed of the creek. Jason took a step, passed me and lobbed a cast up to the head of a narrow stretch of creek about three feet wide. There, the water erupted in a flash of silver scales and white froth and Jason bought a nice rainbow to hand. This one had a deep dark green hue on its back and noticeably more spots across its back and fins compared to the rainbows we had caught the day before.

I cast in the next hole and pulled out a fat little rainbow. These fish were in probably the best condition I had ever seen.

Then we came to a larger slow-moving pool. I've never really liked fishing in them. Working the lures through for one follow-in.

A change of tactics was needed, so I decided to change lures, and both of us tied on the new minnows we had picked up from the tackle store before we left Tamworth.

That day's session on the river would go down as one of the best days fishing I've had. We pulled fish from every single pool. Sometimes multiple fish from the same pools, and we often landed fish at the same time. All fit rainbows. What they lacked in size, they made up for in character.

At one wider hole, shaped like a lily pad, we sat down for a rest but still cast out. The water flowed into the pool off a rock about one foot high and two feet across. It wasn't a large hole, only about 15ft across its widest point. We caught fish on every cast. Jason decided to experiment with the other lures in his box and struggled to find a lure they wouldn't eat.

I felt a pang of regret for not bringing my fly rod. There were no trees or bushes to catch my back cast and these fish seemed very hungry. A wasted opportunity, I thought to myself.

Eventually the fish in that hole wised up, however, and we moved on.

It did start to get a little repetitive, catching these rainbows, and I found myself wishing that there were some brown trout for variety. I suggested to Jason we go back to the car and try another stream.

He agreed, so we drove up out of the nice wide valley and, coming down the next hill, the fog got thicker. You could only see about 100m in front of the car. The descent seemed to end and there was a bridge in front of us. We drove over it slowly to look at the water. It looked even better than the last creek, though there were a lot of short sharp shrubs growing along its banks.

Jason did a U-turn and we parked as far off the road as possible. The car was essentially straddling a table drain, but it was the only safe spot to park.

Rods in hands and bags on backs, we climbed down under the fairly dull modern concrete bridge. The creek was stunningly clear with a slight tannin. It flowed gracefully over the freestone rocks in the bottom. The side we were on had a rocky bank, while the opposite side had a raised grassy bank lined with sharp shrubs. The fog was really thick here and had cut visibility back to around ten meters.

"The last creek had nothing but rainbows," I said to Jason. "Wouldn't it be funny if this creek had nothing but browns?"

I made my first cast under the overhanging bank and hooked a fish. It came to hand very quickly, as it was barely bigger than Jason's partially severed finger. Looking down at the fish in the net, I saw some striking red spots eclipsed with a slightly larger white spot in a straight line along its side. From the lateral line and across, its back was littered with brown spots, and its tail was not blemished by spots. Just a translucent coffee brown. A perfect specimen of a brown trout.

The stream varied greatly in its layout. It had open field on one side, heavy vegetation on the other, whole sections completely locked out by scrub that merged into pockets of rainforest, with large canopy trees over top and ferns lining the steep red clay banks.

We were catching a fish in every hole and having a blast.

We came to a long straight pool only about six feet wide. It was Jason's turn to cast and he hooked what would be the fish of the day. It was a very respectful forty-two centimetre hen brown trout. Not big in the scheme of the global fishing scene, but for here, in this landscape and climate, it was as close to a trophy as you can get.

Jason was wading through the creek while I strode above him on the bank, glancing into the pools of water while he fished. The grass here was a mix of tussock and normal ground cover, but since I was so preoccupied with the pools, I realised too late that my foot was about to hit ground that was not ground at all.

Everything felt like it stood still as I looked in horror at the Tiger snake I was about to crush with my foot. I desperately tried to will my foot back but, as I recoiled backwards, the snake panicked and immediately straightened itself out and plunged off the bank and into the creek. Right in front of Jason!

"SNAKE!" I shouted desperately.

Jason could have been mistaken for Jesus or Peter as he seemed to walk on water to get out of the creek.

The snake disappeared. We had no idea where it went. It splashed into the water and never resurfaced.

Eventually the creek began to taper off. We weren't sure how much further it went, but it was only about a foot wide now and had vines and small trees crisscrossing above the water. One underarm cast, more luck than skill, about 12ft into the chasm of vegetation and the water tension broke as another healthy hen brown came to hand. Without saying a word, knowing it couldn't get better than this, we turned around and headed back to the car.

Popping the car boot, we grabbed some snacks – mainly muesli bars and cheese and crackers – then scoffed them down with some water and planned our next move.

The sun was coming out now and I could feel the intensity of its UV rays on my skin, something I'm sure only red-headed members of the population understand. We shut the boot and once again, headed down under the dull concrete bridge, but this time headed downstream.

We skipped over a large shallow fast-flowing section, and went around a bend. From here the creek dropped about 4ft over a mini waterfall into a large rectangular pool. The water below was shaded even in the heat of the midday sun, thanks to a large canopy of trees, steep rock edges and ferns that grew wherever they could get purchase in the rocks.

"There has to be a big fish in this hole," I said more to myself than out loud, but I had said it out loud and Jason agreed.

So we made our way down to the water edge before casting to the head of the pool and working our lures. There was no immediate luck. Perhaps we were in a bit of midday trance, just casting lures over and over, switching lures occasionally to find out who lived in the hole.

At one point, I stopped my retrieve to glance at Jason's lure, working about 3ft below in the tannin-stained water that almost appeared blue where the light punched through the trees. His little hardbody lure went through a column of sunlight and shimmered up into my eyes. A second later, a bronze flash followed it through. Jason worked the lure to his feet and the brown trout slowly turned away at the bank and headed back into the deep. We never saw it again.

Moving downstream again, we realised that it was very overgrown, fast flowing and shallow. But this was not a downside, without exaggerating we caught a fish in every single hole.

Some of the fish were legal-sized, a lot were smaller than your hand, but all dressed up in striking arrangements of brown and red spots over bronze flanks.

The weather had been a stark contrast to that morning's fog screen, with a vibrant blue sky, occasionally wispy white clouds and a gentle breeze that offset the sun's heat. Bundles of pale grey wood formed log jams that could have been mistaken for a heavy metal band's logo and the fish were always hiding at the base. We had gone downstream a fair distance now, but only been able to fish about half of the water due to the scrub, log jams and spiny bush.

My mind was curious as always, as to just how many fish we actually walked past in those sections. Did they ever see anglers? Or did they just grow big and strong and die of old age? I think

CHAPTER 3 – STREAM HOPPING

I'll put that discussion aside for the philosophers of the world to dwell on.

By mid-afternoon, we had easily brought 100 fish to hand between the two of us. The high from catching so many fish was coming to an end, though, and I could feel my body reminding me of the garbage sleep I'd had the night before. I was about to say I was 'just about done fishing for the day', when Jason said we should probably get going anyways as we had a long drive home.

Cutting our lures off back at the car, before packing away our rods and squaring away our stuff, I slumped into the passenger seat and we drove into the sun, heading back home.

Driving back up the hills that had been blanketed in fog that morning, I was taken back by stunning rolling green hills of cattle farms, subdivided by the silver light of streams reflected in the afternoon light in each valley we passed It was an absolutely stunning part of the world.

I think I dozed off a couple of times, waking as my head knocked on the passenger side window, but whenever I glanced out the window the landscape changed. Pressing my hand on the back of the window, I could feel the crispness of the mountains disappearing and the heat returning.

I was already planning when I could come back.

Old habits die hard and we stopped for some fast food again. It seems to be a vice that young adult males just can't shake. At that point in my life, I'd never not finished a meal, but this burger tasted awful. I slammed it unsympathetically back into the paper bag it came in and snacked on the chips as we made our way back down the New England highway towards Tamworth.

Chapter 4 – Close To Home

I think that bad burger triggered a newfound desire in me to eat less takeaway and do some exercise. So that February, once I finally got a casual job in a bookshop – located in a small arcade in the Tamworth CBD – I started eating fresher food and joined a gym. I made some friends at church, one of whom was Will. Will and his family were some of the most naturally nice and friendly people I would ever meet. They loved God, the Kansas City Chiefs, and the All Blacks – the order of which was up for debate. Will was a touch shorter than me, but built with muscle that showed some of his Māori heritage, and a thick moustache on his top lip, something that I as a 17-year-old was not capable of growing without a gentle breeze blowing it away.

The gym was in the old Tamworth Workman's Club, which even then was fastly becoming dilapidated. It had a shopping mall style undercover car park, and directly underneath the club's heated pool a large puddle of water was constantly topped up by a drip through the concrete above.

One day, Will and I were lifting weights when some older guys working out nearby started talking about fishing. "I caught some nice trout up at the flags on the weekend..." one of the bald gym junkies said.

I continued lifting weights like I hadn't heard it. But, as soon as they moved off to a separate area of the gym, Will told me about a place where they'd caught some cracking rainbows close to home. He had my undivided attention. "How far away is it?" I asked.

He looked around and whispered, "It's only half an hour from here."

Walking back down the steps of the gym and into the dusty drippy carpark, a small flock of pigeons that had been roosting on a water pipe against the concrete roof flew off rapidly. They did a loop outside before landing again.

"We can go up to this spot today, if you're free this afternoon?" Will suggested.

I immediately agreed and he said he would pick me up around 3pm.

Back home, I showered, then gathered up my fishing gear and dumped it in a pile. I had my little spin rod and also my fly rod. "Just in case they are biting," I said to myself.

Then, at exactly 3pm, I stepped out the door of our unit and stood on the concrete step. The sun was out and, with the dry heat of the Tamworth summer, that made it feel like stepping into

CHAPTER 4 – CLOSE TO HOME

an oven. Luckily, the faint rumble of an engine soon sounded, followed by gravel crunching together, as Will pulled up into the driveway. My gear was loaded into the boot of the silver sedan and we headed off.

Half an hour later, we turned onto a small gravel road and rolled down toward the Macdonald River. Great stands of casuarinas, willows and gums formed opposing walls beside the river, cloaking it in shadow. We parked ourselves under the shade of trees on some larger river rocks, then got our gear ready.

The Macdonald River starts its journey around the village of Niangala, before converging and becoming the Namoi river in the heart of Warrabah National Park. The water here, though, varied in width and flow, passing over a mix of large granite boulders both in and out of the water. The base of the river then also varied between coarse sand and river stones, giving the water a slight tannin stain.

Still, I put on my thigh waders, rigged up my spin rod and tied on my personal favourite 'prospecting lure' – the black and copper spinner. It was my favourite because, even if the trout didn't bite, they often followed it in, revealing their presence in the river. Then I stood patiently on the right bank of the river, facing upstream, about a one-foot drop from the hole above where water cascaded over multiple large black boulders. The turbulent water then entered the pool, creating a bubble line that swept over to the left bank, in a deeper section of the river that hugged a slightly undercut clay bank with yabby holes – it looked like a block of Swiss cheese.

I focused on the water coming in and flipped the bail arm over while pinching onto the braided line with my index finger against the cork grip. I pointed the rod tip behind me and flicked forward, gently lifting my index finger off the cork and letting the line flow freely behind the spinner headed to the top of the hole. It let out a gentle 'plop' sound as it broke through the surface tension, and I flipped the bail arm back over and began winding immediately.

My lure thrummed as it worked through the water via my rod's sensitive graphite tip, but then momentarily the thrumming ceased and the rod tip dipped and darted in harmony with the trout that had clearly taken a liking to it. I gently coaxed the trout up into the shallow water pockets among all the fist-sized river rocks, then reached down and picked it up with my hand.

This little hen rainbow was more silver than its Ebor cousins, and was only around twenty centimetres in length, rounded out in the belly like a football from obviously feeding on lots of something. It was too small to keep (given the legal size was twenty-five centimetres in New South Wales), however, so I gently unhooked it and nudged it back into the river.

After a few tail kicks on a downward trajectory, it disappeared into the current.

As the afternoon went on, I brought a few more clones of the first fish to hand, then decided to do something I hadn't yet attempted – to catch a river trout on my fly rod. After cutting the spinner off and putting it back in the tackle box, then winding up the slack line onto the reel and looping it into the line stopper, I pulled the three sections of my rod apart, put them back into the car and pulled out my bulky beginners five-to-six weight. It was the cheapest rod I could afford at that time, which, like everything in life, meant it was in no way comparable in quality to more expensive rods.

Still, I lined up the guides on the three sections of the rod, then pinched a loop of the fly line and brought it up through the guides. I was now faced with a decision that I had no idea how to make, as I stared into a box full of random flies I'd accumulated from different shops. "Are they really that fussy?" I thought to myself, given they just ate a couple of spinning bits of metal.

A magazine advertisement I had recently seen for a fly line said something like "98% of a trout's diet is under the surface". With that in mind, I picked out a random black bead head nymph, tied it onto the end of my tippet and walked back up to the same hole.

Once there, I stripped out arms lengths of the yellow fly line into coils in the water in front of my feet. I began moving the line backwards and forwards, then backwards again, though the line unfortunately pulled up tight as my fly snagged itself in a bunch of hanging willow branches behind me.

Spending the next five minutes untangling the mess and unsnagging the fly, I was soon ready to make another cast. I managed to lay the line out relatively straight but it didn't go where I wanted it. Intently watching the line, and the end of my yellow line to see if it dipped at all, it drifted all the way down the run.

Nothing.

I repeated the dance of getting stuck in the trees and making horrible casts for about an hour before winding up the line and going to see how Will was fairing.

Past the car and two pools down, I found Will sitting on the bank. He had had a few hits and follows, but none brought to hand.

Then I heard a noise. It was subtle, but something had broken the water. Scanning the surface, I heard the noise again and saw a trout partially leap out of the water to intercept one of the many caddis floating in a flurry just above.

I quickly waded out into the sandy bottomed river and, when the water was about three inches from coming into my waders, I stopped and began making casts towards the location of the rising fish.

A waning gibbous moon was now lighting the world below, turning the river silver and black, the bubble line unmistakably contrasted. It was beautiful. Even more so as the trout rose again while I was humming a tune in my head, in a state of catharsis, letting anything I was holding onto float downstream. I felt so weightless standing there, feeling the cool chill of the river against my legs, yet knowing I was dry.

Then something happened that didn't take me by surprise, but I wasn't really expecting it to happen either – as I went to pull

CHAPTER 4 – CLOSE TO HOME

in the slack to maintain my constant drift, the line jarred in my hand before slipping back out. The trout then made a series of jumps across the moonlit water, breaking the beat of the frogs and choir of the crickets. I didn't need to measure her to know she was undersized like the others, and I also had no intention of keeping her, so with a wet hand and keeping her in the water I twisted the hook out of her mouth and she disappeared into the black.

Climbing out of the river in the dark that day, I knew I wasn't the same man who had walked in.

Chapter 5 – On My Own
March 2009

That March was unusually warm for the beginning of our autumn here in Australia, but one morning I felt hotter than usual... as I was waiting to take my provisional drivers' license test – a practical examination that, if passed, would allow me to drive on my own. I was so nervous that, even though I had just finished in the shower and was brushing my teeth, sweat formed above my brow.

The car I was taking my test in was a 1976 Toyota Corolla – freshly painted dark green, with only one side mirror on the driver's side by design. The interior was a dull dusty brown and there was a medallion of Saint Christopher stuck on the dash from the previous owner. It didn't feel particularly safe – and I guess that's why the last owners put the medallion in – but it had a lot of character and had been good to learn to drive in, with its four-speed manual gearbox.

At the test centre, a middle-aged lady with slightly grey blonde hair and wearing a fluorescent yellow safety vest emerged from the single-storey brick building and signalled for me to place my L-plates on the vehicle. Then we inspected the vehicle's exterior

CHAPTER 5 – ON MY OWN

together, going over the tyres and mirrors, amongst other things. I explained that it only had the one side mirror by design, but for the purpose of the test I would pretend that it had one on the passenger side as well, for the sake of doing my head checks during the examinations. She nodded in agreement.

So I climbed into the hot interior of the car, and reached over to unlock the passenger door so she could get in. I apologised that the car had no air conditioning, but she should feel free to open and shut her window as necessary.

I was, quite frankly, a nervous wreck, already certain this assessor was notorious for failing people over small things, according to the rumours. I remembered some advice a family friend had given me, saying that he had made a bunch of mistakes during his own test, but had just made conversation the whole time and guessed that made them not as observant.

So, just as we were about to leave the carpark and I opened my mouth to make conversation, I realised that I wouldn't be able to – my mouth felt like the desert had swept in, my throat dried out into a wasteland and my saliva glands had stopped working. I coughed a little in panic. I didn't even have a bottle of water in the car – I was going to choke to death because I still had forty-five minutes of the test left!

So I focussed my breathing and kept my mouth shut, hoping I could at least make enough saliva to stop me from choking again. Luckily, a few blocks down the road, I was back to normal and decided to start up a conversation. I can't remember what it was about, but I did my best to distract her.

After we returned to the carpark and she got out of the car, I reached over to lock the door after her, then climbed out myself, locked my door with the key, and went inside.

I sat for what felt like forever. The constant calling of numbers that weren't mine kept me on edge, until I was second-guessing everything I had done in the test.

But then finally my number was called out and I was told to stand against a white board and look at the camera. I crack a half-baked smile, not realising that this wouldn't be allowed next time I renewed my license, then the assessor emerged from behind the counter and ran me through the results.

"Your angle park was bad, and you missed two head checks when you were first at the lights. If you had missed three head checks you would have failed, but you've passed! Congratulations."

I was so happy! So I thanked her and she told me to take a seat while my license got made up. When I eventually stepped out of the building and into the midday sun, I held a white and red card in one hand and in the other hand a pile of white square plates with a large red P in the middle. This was the beginning of my independence.

CHAPTER 5 – ON MY OWN

Although I was never a good early riser, for something I wanted to do I could make the odd exception. The next day, I didn't have to start work at the bookshop until 10:30am, so I set my alarm for 6am so I could drive up to The Great Dividing Range and be on the water by around 6:50am when the sun was set to rise.

Still, I got a shock when my alarm broke the silence in our unit, gasping before slapping the off button and climbing out of bed. I grabbed my spin rod from the corner of the room, my waders, and a box full of trout lures, slid them into my old school bag, zipped it up and headed for the car.

It was still dark out, the sky was clear, and it was a beautiful crisp autumn morning. The gravel of the driveway crunched underneath the tyres as I reversed out of our driveway and into the laneway. Flagstaff mountain was a beautiful dark silhouette, wrapping its ridges around the street lights below. I took a left turn and drove east until I hit the roundabout on the New England highway, which only had a gentle hum of traffic, none of the sirens or road raging car horns of peak hour.

The sun was close to rising when I arrived at the spot. I pulled up under the same row of trees as I had done before, hopped out of the car, pulled on my waders, tied on a lure, locked the car and began to make my way downstream. Dew glistened silver on the grass surrounding the river bank, while a gentle breeze whooshed through the shea oaks creating an almost eerie ambience. Freedom never felt so good.

I found myself at a promising hole in the river that seemed very wide and deep, so scrambled down the eroded river bank and onto some large granite boulders rocks towards the tail end of the pool. I started fanning casts around the hole with little to no interest, but I couldn't complain – the morning light was stunning and, after about ten minutes, a platypus gently broke through the surface of the river and gently suspended itself before duck-diving back into the water.

I cast and cast and cast and watched the sun rise higher above the hills in the East, I knew I had to start thinking about heading back to get to work on time. But then I was drawn back to what I was doing as a nice legal-sized rainbow trout took my lure!

The fish had vibrant purple cheeks and a scattering of freckled spots with a beautiful pink stripe along the lateral line. I decided to keep this fish to make Mum happy, and also to examine its stomach contents to better understand the diet of these fish.

Rod in one hand and a quickly dispatched trout in the other, I scrambled back up the eroded bank and meandered back along the western bank of the river towards the car. When I was almost back at the car, though, I realised I couldn't feel my keys pressing into my leg from my pocket anymore. I immediately set down my rod and fish and began frisking my legs through my waders, only to confirm my suspicions – my keys were gone.

I shot a glance back towards the river, thinking of any possible places they could have fallen out. The only place was where I had scrambled down and back up the eroded bank. So I hurried all the

CHAPTER 5 – ON MY OWN

way back to the bank and began looking on the ground – with no sign of the keys. Defeated, I turned back to the car and started to plan what I would do now, as the spare keys were back at home and I was up the mountain on my own.

But as I approached the rear of my car, I looked at the door and noticed something – my keys were still in the door! In all my haste to be on the water, I'd locked the car and just left the keys hanging out of the lock. Just as well it was a quiet spot and not in town!

Driving back down the mountain was always so much more enjoyable, as my little 4-speed Corolla could reach the speed limit without straining, and my music didn't have to compete with any revs.

Once at home, I pulled back into the driveway, quickly unloaded my gear, put the trout in the fridge to deal with later, changed into my work clothes, then head straight back out the door so I wasn't late for work. All day, however, I kept thinking back to my fish, my mind unable to leave the river.

Finally home from work, I slapped the trout onto a chopping board and got out my fillet knife. I first made a cut under the gills, before taking the knife into the vent just before the anal fin and cutting back towards the head where I had made the first incision. Then I placed the knife down and, with my index and middle finger, pushed into the back of the gut cavity, before hooking my fingers and bringing them forward in the same direction as the cut. With the guts then on the chopping board, I grabbed the gills and twisted them out. A quick run with the back of my thumbnail down the spine, visible in the gut cavity, to remove the kidney trapped under a fine membrane, and the job was done.

Taking my fillet knife now, I grabbed the fish's light pink stomach from the gut pile and noticed it was pretty full – this fish had been eating a lot! I cut the stomach lengthways and, about thirty to fifty identically sized insects spilled out!

They were damsel nymphs, each about twenty millimetres long, rich dark brown in colour.

Time to cook now, I prepared the trout in about the only way I knew how, stuffing the gut cavity with lemon slices and butter before placing it onto aluminium foil, along with more butter and lemon. I made the final wraps of the foil and placed it in the oven for twenty minutes. Once cooked, the lemon butter smell would erupt from the foil in a dance of steam and fill the unit. It was a good honest meal and Mum was glad I'd finally brought home a fish rather than playing with them and throwing them back.

After tidying up the kitchen, I went back to my room, opened up my fly box, and to my surprise there were a half dozen damsel nymph flies in there too, both brown and olive, matching the size of the ones inside the trout's stomach.

The next day, I would go fishing again, this time after work.

Chapter 6 – Cracking the Code

As soon as my bookshop shift finished the next day, I power-walked to my car, parked one and a half city blocks away, texting my friend Mike to come and join me for a fish. I told him to be ready in half an hour.

Back home I ran into the house, changed, grabbed my fishing gear and fly rod, and headed back out the door. I decided to bring my spin rod as well, but that was purely for Mike to use.

It was about mid-afternoon now and we were powering up the hill in my little Corolla, blaring out a track mix of Underoath and Haste the Day, and just all round having a good time.

The drive went fast and, almost like a ritual now, I turned down the dirt road to the wall of trees flanking the river and parked in the shade on the loose river stones. We probably only had an hour until sunset, but we were determined to make the most of it.

I set the spin rod up for Mike with a spinner, then set up my fly rod with the damsel fly. I locked the car, made sure to place the keys in my pocket this time, and we headed downstream.

We made a beeline straight for the largest hole on that section of river and climbed down the steep bank. Mike stayed on a set of rocks on the water's edge and began casting into the big deep hole. Whereas I jumped across the tailwater of the pool, my feet landing firmly on a large granite boulder, about the same area as the roof of my car. Clearly I wasn't the only one who had taken a liking to that boulder, as it was peppered with duck droppings.

We cast and we cast and we cast.

Nothing.

It was still warm but the sun was creeping slowly behind the gums on the ridgeline.

Then all of a sudden, about 15ft out from my boulder, the otherwise still water was disrupted by a dinner-plate sized boil in the water. I quickly stripped my line in and cast to where the water was boiling, before it returned to glass.

My damsel fly landed with a gentle 'plonk' sound, I took the line in my hand and made a long steady strip. I was about halfway through the second strip of line, when the line slipped back out of my hand. I instinctively raised my rod tip and felt the unmistakable pull of a trout on the other end. I brought it right to the edge of my boulder, then realised I had forgotten my landing net! With a foot drop from the boulder to the water, I didn't want to risk lifting the fish with the light tippet material, so hesitated.

And in that moment of indecision, the little rainbow shook itself free of my hook and disappeared into the dark water, leaving a boil of disappointment behind on the surface.

The sun then set, but the placid glass surface of the large hole was soon replaced by the boils of trout entering into a feeding

CHAPTER 6 – CRACKING THE CODE

frenzy – the second hatch I would ever witness. Every cast I made towards these rising fish resulted in a hookup, and the action was non-stop for what felt like an hour, though was probably only ten to fifteen minutes. I dropped another four fish before landing a solid plate-sized rainbow to bring home for Mum.

Afterwards, Mike looked at me and said, "I'm never coming with you again unless you bring a net."

We both laughed and, with the action now over, began the walk back to the car in the dark, tripping over loose stones and tufts of tussock grass.

Two days later, I decided to head back. I rounded up some gear and dug my landing net out of the garage. I called Mike again. "Hey Mike, want to chase some trout again?" to which he replied sarcastically, "Not if you don't have a landing net." We had a good laugh and made plans.

The drive and the river were now very familiar to me, like visiting a relative's house. After we pulled up on the loose river stones, under the shade of the trees, we made our way straight to the big pool.

We again made cast after cast after cast. Nothing. But as the sun began to set below the horizon, the water again came to life with hungry trout. Mike tried a few different lures on the spin gear but couldn't even get a strike. I once again cast the damsel nymph fly towards the rising trout and was rewarded with tight lines and fish to hand.

There was clearly no shortage of fish in this large pool, as evidenced by the sheer number of them rising simultaneously. Mike's old man had requested a few for dinner, so I was happy to keep a couple and carefully released the rest.

We had finally cracked the code for these fish.

At least for now.

Chapter 7 – Full Submersion
October 2009

It was a week before the October long weekend and I was talking to my older brother Mark about fishing the trout opening day at Ebor. I was really keen to get back into the Guy Fawkes River below the falls, now that any recollections of Jason and my suffering had faded into pleasant memories of fish and wild country.

We formulated a very adolescent plan that involved leaving Tamworth late at night after Mark finished work on Friday, 'parking' at the lookout carpark while we 'shut our eyes' before setting off down the slopes first thing the next morning.

So that Friday came and I heard the familiar crunch of tyres on the gravel driveway and knew Mark had arrived. I wasted no time and threw my gear into the back of his Silver Mitsubishi Magna, climbed into the passenger seat and we headed north in the dark, listening to a few heavy metal albums from Demon Hunter and Living Sacrifice to stay awake, and to talk Mark through what he needed to know come sunrise.

The music seemed to match the weather as we got closer to Ebor – the sky darkening with clouds and the rain starting to pour. We turned off the highway into a thick white fog bank, dashes of vibrant raindrops illuminated against the fog came down sideways all around the car, before being absorbed into the lichen-covered bitumen.

It was just after midnight when I finally reached into the backseat for my sleeping bag, took off my shoes, reclined the passenger seat and curled up to sleep. Even with the car lights now off, the thick cloud sky was a luminous grey and I watched as branches of the overhanging eucalypts seemingly wrestled each other, the wind stirring them on.

I don't really remember being asleep, but I do remember waking and noticing the clock had moved forward on the small green-figured dash clock. I wasn't sure if it was the close space, my almost upright sleeping position, or the excitement of the day to come that stopped me from sleeping soundly but I'm willing to blame all of them.

The only benefit of not sleeping for long periods of time was the almost guarantee that I would not sleep through my alarm. So when I opened my eyes and saw the grey of the coming dawn through the trees to the east, I disabled the alarm on my phone and gave a now-snoring Mark a loving shove through his sleeping bag.

After stashing away my sleeping bag into its carry bag, I put my shoes back on, climbed out of the car and gave my body a bit of stretch, hoping it wouldn't make me pay for the discomfort I had forced it through over the previous five hours.

CHAPTER 7 – FULL SUBMERSION

The rain had at least stopped falling, though there seemed to be a perpetual mist blowing around in the predawn sky.

While I had started to crack the code on the rainbow trout close to home, this spot had always had its murky water challenges and I'd never cast a fly into it, so wasn't sure how well a fly would do down here. Which led me to take my three-piece travel rod, as well as my three-piece five-to-six weight rod.

I rigged up the spin rod with my always faithful black and copper Celta, stashed my other rod into the side of my old school bag and walked to the edge of the hill.

"Like I told you," I said to Mark, "it's hard to grasp just how steep this is without standing right here and looking over."

A look of doubt came over his face, the same doubt I had experienced when standing in this exact spot with Jason.

I answered his wordless question with, "Trust me, it's worth it."

The falls thundered as ever in the background, with all the fresh fury of an extra inch or two of water from the overnight downpour. We cautiously made our way down the sodden face, grasping razor grass and tactically sliding down sections on our asses, each step and each slide bringing us closer to the river.

When the river came into view, we pushed past the final edge of vegetation and stepped out onto the lichen-covered rocks. The first hole we came to was one of the larger pockets of water in this stretch of the river, and there was an obvious inflow of water coming in between the gap of two boulders at the head. I lobbed the Celta right up into the whitewater and was all but instantly rewarded with a fighting fit hen rainbow trout. We took a couple of photos on my phone, released her gently, and she took off furiously.

I told Mark to keep fishing while I switched rods. I packed down the spin rod and set up the bulky fly rod. I opened up my little fly box and plucked out a #12 black bead head nymph that I had tied myself on a borrowed fly tying vise that a friend had lent me. Then I stripped a handful of yellow line from the reel and began to make a series of false casts to the head of the pool.

I watched the end of that yellow line like a hawk, looking for any sign of movement that might betray the prey below. I made a few more of the same casts with no interest. I was almost ready to move onto the next pool when I noticed a subtle secondary bubble line. It was almost invisible, except for a few pieces of off-white foam occasionally coming into its current.

Then I realised what was happening – water from upstream was flowing under a big square boulder at the head of the pool, not over the top, so it wasn't obvious to see where this second line originated from but it was definitely there. One, two, three false casts later, and the nymph dropped into the water mere inches from the face of the boulder.

The flow wasn't as fast as the main channel, which let the nymph drop down deeper into the murky pool. I saw the tip of the fly line move to the right, lifted the rod, and my heart almost sank, thinking I'd set the hook into a snag and would now lose my fly. My heart lurched forward at the same time that the trout on

CHAPTER 7 – FULL SUBMERSION

the other end of the line realised something about his last choice of meal, not being entirely fit for consumption.

A very acrobatic buck rainbow burst through the nutrient rich water and momentarily broke the constant sound of the thunderous falls behind. This was a good fish, actually still the biggest fish I'd ever seen come from this section of water. He had spots all over and a big hook jaw, well into the 40-50cm bracket, and had obviously never passed up a meal in its life, judging from his broad shoulders and condition. A few snaps on the phone and I released him to fight another day, before replacing my phone into its zip-lock bag and placing it in the pocket of my jeans.

By now the rain had started back again, so Mark and I put on our raincoats and thought about making sure Mark got a few fish on the board.

I'd loaned Mark my 1-3kg rod, which I had used down here on that first trip with Jason; and in the next pool, despite the rain, Mark landed a nice healthy rainbow. I'm almost certain that this was one of Mark's first river-caught trout. We had caught plenty of trout growing up from the Sheba Dams up in the mountains, and even a few fish from Lake Jindabyne on our occasional summer holidays to the Snowy Mountains, but here and now these were special fish. Wild and mostly untouched.

It was a sensational morning of fishing, and I was absolutely cleaning up on my hand-tied fly. Mark was slaying fish on the spin gear. The ecstasy of it all almost drowned out all our slipping on wet rocks, busted shins and the overall miserable weather hanging around.

We had been making our way downstream and were now further than Jason and I had ever made it that first time. The valley walls became steeper here, and the boulders between steps of the river grew taller. There was really no safe way to get down further – the size of the boulders were massive and the almost vertical walls made walking around unviable.

So we sat atop a large moss covered boulder next to the river, and I slid off my backpack to pull out some snacks while we discussed our next move.

Below us was a 4m vertical drop. To our left was a gap in between some boulders – very narrow but maybe wide enough that we might be able to shimmy our way down inside to reach the section below. To our right was the main current of the river. Then, directly below us, was an outcrop of jagged rocks pointing towards us like an army of soldiers with bayonets. Beyond the frontline of defensive rocks was a pile of foam about a foot tall, and beyond it were more jagged rocks.

"You really don't want to risk falling down there!" I said to Mark.

But, as he looked over, the foam below parted as the shoulders of a feeding trout pushed it aside. Mark and I looked at each other in disbelief, then I simply reached over and grabbed my rod, stripped off some line and lowered it down into the foot-sized gap in the off-white foam.

CHAPTER 7 – FULL SUBMERSION

The fly found its way beyond the troops of rocks and into the black water. I felt a tug on the line and reflexively leaned back while raising the rod tip to set the hook. It was a big mistake.

During the unexpected bite, I had thrust my hips forward and the slippery moss below my butt betrayed me... and sent me hurtling towards my death!

Time is a fascinating beast. You might scroll on your phone for thirty minutes and think that only a minute has passed by. Or you might hold a plank position for hours, only to realise it was a mere fifteen seconds. Or you could be in my shoes sliding off a boulder, and in the 0.9035 seconds it takes you to fall, you can have enough time to reflect on your whole life, to say a little prayer, and to think about how you'll only leave the river that day in a body bag or a stretcher. Either way, it would be the first day you get to go in a helicopter. For me, I just wished it had been under better circumstances.

I'd been falling for years of course, so decided to aim for the tiny patch of parted foam where the trout had been. I could tell the water wouldn't be deep from looking at all the jagged rocks, and knew I'd likely break my legs on impact. But if I could just lean forward, I'd hopefully avoid smashing my head against those damn jagged rocks.

Every single sensory input to my body was flooded, though – I could still hear the sound of the changing pitch of the river as I got closer to my fate: the smell of moss, freshly moved dirt and wet eucalyptus. I could see the rocks and water rising to swallow me and mutilate me beyond measure.

It was all too much.

I shut my eyes and accepted my fate.

The world went dark, cold and silent. I was suspended between this world and the next. I opened my eyes and everything was black. I was struggling to come to terms with what was happening but, from above, there was a ray of brown light beaming through the clouds. I raised my hands and pushed them down, the air felt heavy and cold. I wondered if this was what birds felt as they flapped their wings.

This realm was strange and the distant clouds were now close to my fingertips.

Then I broke through the clouds and gasped for air.

Water was now dripping from my hair and across my face. The roar of the river came back as the shock faded and water drained from my ears. The sky was still grey with clouds overhead. I lay half in the water and half on the rocks. I looked up and saw a blurry figure hurrying towards me. He was saying something – I could tell from his lips moving – but I couldn't hear what it was.

"Are you alright?" I think Mark said.

CHAPTER 7 – FULL SUBMERSION

I pulled myself from the water and up onto the rocks, gingerly tapping my limbs and looking for cuts in my clothing, though I couldn't see anything. Then I remembered my new phone was in my pocket and quickly pulled it out of my wet clothes. Thankfully it wasn't broken and still inside the zip-lock bag – what a good lifehack that had turned out to be!

My lucky blaze-orange Remington hat was gone, though, and so was my fly rod. I wasn't overly disappointed in this as I would now have an excuse to upgrade my fly rod!

Still, I turned back to the pool I had plunged into and took it all in – it was barely four to five feet in diameter but somehow deeper than two metres, as I had never hit the bottom. I looked around for any sign of my hat, then about a foot below the surface was the cork grip of my fly rod. I reached down, grabbed it, and started to strip the slack line up. Once I had all the slack line back under control, something happened... The fish was still on the other end of the line!

I was in utter disbelief as I bent down and brought the solid hen rainbow to hand. I grabbed a rock from below my feet and dashed her over the head and she went still in my hands. I turned to Mark and said, "If I'm going to almost die for a fish, there is no way I'm releasing it."

I packed the fish into my old school bag, and took my rod back to the pool to see if I could push it down enough and find my hat. Flat on my belly at the edge of the pool, I pushed the nine-foot rod-down into the dark water and, to my surprise, could not even touch the bottom. Giving my lucky hat up for lost, I accepted losing it to the river was a much better situation than myself becoming lost to the river.

There was a problem, though. Not an immediate one, but one I knew would become a problem if I didn't sort it out... My clothes were completely saturated and I had no spares, not even in the car.

So I stripped down to my underwear and started ringing the murky water from my jeans, button-up fishing shirt and camo jacket. It made puddles at the base of the overhanging boulder, which I was standing under as a windbreak. Knowing everything was still really saturated, I put my jeans and shirt back on, but tied my jacket around my waist, hoping it would allow itself and my shirt to dry simultaneously.

Of course, looking at the misty rain still putting a lid over the gorge and completely obscuring the sun, I didn't like my chances.

Chapter 8 – Delayed Drying

We decided to keep fishing a bit further down below the boulder where I had fallen. It turned out to be the right choice, as I brought another half dozen beautiful rainbow trout to hand over a stretch of about one hundred metres. We came across a similar drop off with high gorge walls and decided that we would turn around here and make our way back.

Spotting a ridge that looked to be not as vertical and heading in the direction of the lookout, we ascended from the valley floor, slipping on loose rocks and gaining purchase on any tuft of grass or plant we could find.

The thick cloud skyline between the gums gradually looked closer. Then we came across some sheer vertical rock faces that I'm sure a rock climbing or bouldering group would be chuffed with, but I was not.

So we now had to traverse around the side of the hill until we were closer to the lookout and pretty much came up on our hands and knees at the place where we first went down.

Back on top of the mountain, the wind was relentless and a sideways drizzle blew across the landscape, which probably explained the various mosses and lichens growing on almost every tree in the lookout area.

Mark asked me how I was feeling, knowing that I didn't have any dry clothes and there were no towels in the car. I looked at him and said, "I actually want to go and catch some brown trout."

He gave me that older and wiser look of 'probably not the best idea but it's your choice'.

So we climbed into the magna and headed east for the streams between Ebor and Dorrigo.

To my surprise, the grey clouds were starting to illuminate, and in a few places thick rays of light were even shining down and illuminating the lush green grass of the surrounding farms.

I was feeling cold and wet, but knew that a few hours of sun could at least dry me out enough to enjoy the trip home. We pulled off the road at the same stream Jason and I had come to before, and left the car parked precariously over the top of a drain, grabbed our rods and headed down to the water.

There was a thick fog over the creek, which was often the case on these streams, and as soon as I popped my head over the edge of the bank under the bridge I saw bow waves across the water from the tail of the pool. I even saw a pair of fish thrash through the rapids at the head of the pool and rage across the next pool.

CHAPTER 8 – DELAYED DRYING

"That was weird," I said to Mark, turning back around to see if he had seen the fish.

He nodded.

We quickly bypassed the first two holes and, as soon as we put a cast into the third pool, we saw the fish spook and torpedo for the head of the pool, where they disappeared. Not really wanting to give up on our chances of getting a 'New England Slam' we pressed on to the next few holes and received a similar reception.

The sun had completely disappeared by now, and the sideways drizzle had finally caught back up to us.

"I'm pretty sure this place has been fished hard today already," I told Mark. "I've never seen the fish so flighty, even on an overcast day like today."

He agreed, so we made our way back to the Magna, taking a slightly different route. On the way, we noticed footprints in the mud that confirmed our suspicions.

Disgruntled, I packed down my rod, took off my shoes, threw them in the large boot of the sedan, then awkwardly scrambled across the sharp gravel to climb in the passenger seat.

We drove for about an hour before the sun went down, and the whole time I had the air vents set to blow air hard into the footwell – I was doing my best to thaw and dry out, but my wet jeans and shirt were still soaking wet. My teeth began to chatter, and I'm sure if I were to look back over my first aid course notes, I'd be in the early stages of hypothermia.

True to every trip we made this way, the allure of fast food was too much to resist, and I was in dire need of something warm. Our selected takeaway restaurant handed us a cardboard cup tray with a couple of large coffees, a rolled-up paper bag with some burgers, and we were back on the road, heading down from The Great Dividing Range to Tamworth.

I held the coffee in my hands to let its warmth radiate, and with every sip I started to feel human again, even though all things considered it was probably the worst coffee I had ever tasted.

By the time we rounded the hill and saw the lights of Tamworth, I worked out that I had spent close to 12 hours soaking wet, many of those in single digit temperatures.

Mark dropped me off at home, I put my trout in the fridge and headed straight for a hot shower. Then I all but collapsed into bed, curled up in the fetal position, and sleep took me away.

Chapter 9 – The Little Styx

October - December 2010

By now, I had become absolutely addicted to trout. I began to research new fishing spots around Ebor, and found an accommodation website that offered old logging cabins with no electricity, but with running water, gas hot water, showers, toilets, and they were pretty cheap per night, especially split between a few people.

I called Jason and told him about it. When I mentioned that the cabins were right on the water and we wouldn't have to climb down a hill to reach the trout, he was in on a new adventure. A phone call to my older brother Mark and we had a plan – I made a booking for 27 December for three nights.

Everything seemed to move at a snail's pace for the rest of the year, counting down the days until we left. The wait was killing me. I tried to distract myself with no success, so instead decided to dive headfirst into preparing.

I started tying flies, mainly simple ties like black bead head nymphs and e-scouting maps.

Diving into the maps, I realised that the river flowing past the cabins was the Little Styx River, which eventually flowed over some falls and became the Styx River.

Some further searching revealed that the Styx River was one of the most picturesque trout streams in Australia, and from the few photos available online I could see what they meant. There weren't many photos, though, so for the most part we were going in blind.

The 27th finally approached. I spent the day before packing and double checking all my gear, making sure it was all ready to go. Mark and I went to the tackle store to pick up some leader material and a few other bits and pieces of camping equipment we were missing.

On the day itself, Jason was running late. I was just about to call him when his silver ute pulled into the car park and he climbed out of the passenger seat, his dad behind the wheel. Dressed in a black three-piece suit, with bed hair and pale skin, it was plain to see that he had been at the boxing day races and had had a really good time, for which he was now paying the price.

Regardless, we quickly loaded our gear into the back of his ute, while he changed out of his suit and into some more fishing friendly attire, and once Jason's mum arrived to collect his chauffeur, we set off.

We were at least an hour into the trip before he said a word, and even then it wasn't much. He was too hungover for even light conversation.

CHAPTER 9 – THE LITTLE STYX

Eventually, we saw signs for Point Lookout Road and to the trout hatchery, made a right turn, and swapped the smooth bitumen for corrugations, potholes and loose gravel.

The sky was bright blue, little to no wind, and outside we could hear the steady rhythmic song of cicadas up high in the gums. We passed a few creeks without signs, then also the Serpentine Creek. Water was gently lapping over the weir on its eastern side before going through a culvert under the road and flowing west under a small bridge and on through the trout hatchery. It wasn't a particularly stunning stream but it was a large body of water for this part of the world and was a good murky grey colour.

The ute hopped, skidded and jumped through a series of potholes as we traversed the gravel road, around a corner and down a steep hill. The road beyond was shielded by the canopy of gums but, as we descended lower, the scenery opened up. To the east, there was a nice open pasture with a small serpentine-like creek weaving its way up to the hill beyond where cattle browsed lazily. Then, crossing a box culvert, we got our first glimpse of the Little Styx River. Its water was clear and dark.

We found the seldom-used track down to the cabins on the right and made our way down.

There were two old logging cabins, almost identical to one another. The outside walls were a shade of red with moss and lichen taking hold in places. Their front façades appeared to have later extensions, as they were not as tall and the short eaves had allowed water to trickle down and stain the wooden planks a rustic black. A few large green ferns were growing up near the small entrance to our cabin, tucked in around the rusty tin chimney.

The mountain air was fresh and earthy, and the river song could be heard close to the opposite side of the cabin. It seemed like heaven. We found the keys already in the door to our cabin ironically named 'Hilton', so we turned them and swung the old door open, which let out a creaking noise.

To the right was a small bathroom with gas hot water for the shower, and straight ahead opened up into a living area with a large cylindrical iron hearth. Red and white cloth drapes adorned a generously sized off-white window, which illuminated the exposed timber planks stacked horizontally for the internal walls. Beyond that was a bunk room with mattresses, with no linen on them, and back to the left of the hearth was a small kitchen made up of open-face cupboards, a sink and a beautiful enamel wood fired oven. It was simple, rustic and in its own way charming.

We unloaded our gear from the car and dumped it in the living area, before we quickly got our fishing gear together to make the most of the afternoon. We could organise the rest later.

I pulled on some khaki PVC chest waders, put my three-piece five-to-six weight together, ensured the guides lined up nicely before pinching the fly line over and threading it up through the guides. Searching through my fly box and thinking back to a documentary I had watched, 'A River Somewhere' (1997), I found a Royal Humpy fly in a size 14 and tied it onto the end of the tippet. Mark and Jason were likewise finishing the last of their knots when I finally looked up, ready to go. Jason had his spin rod and Mark had his new fly rod.

The plan was to get as far downstream as we could and fish our way back upstream to the cabin.

To the west of the cabins, we found a bit of a game trail through the scrub and began to bash through the surprisingly dense scrub. There was a small clearing in amongst it, and the remains of some old stone wall, most of which was claimed back by the wild with thick moss and lichen growth.

Slowly, the rumbling of the river got louder and louder, and when we came out of the mess of vines and ferns lining the bank we found a giant cascade of water. It was absolutely belting down an almost forty-five-degree angle slope of jagged rocks, a loud and violent mess of white and dark cold water. The moss and lichen growth was thick on all of the nearby overhanging vines and rocks, clearly spurred to growth by the moisture-rich environment.

The first pool upstream was stunning, crisp cool dark water framed inside lush ferns, vines and moss-covered dark rocks. Mark went to make a cast and became stuck in some low hanging branches. I quickly realised that this was going to be a challenging place to fish. So while Mark fished this pool with Jason, I opted to fish a pool slightly further up where I could get into the river itself, and hopefully make a back cast without becoming tangled with the scrub.

As I stepped into the water, the pressure of the current pressed solidly around my calf muscles and the water's chill radiated through my waders shortly after. I was soon just below a series of boulders that divided the pools in front of me with a step formation.

My target pool was about waist-deep, dark and clear. The water flowing into that pool came through a gap between two large boulders and formed a bubble line that stretched back towards me, about twelve feet or so in length. Mark and Jason walked upstream straight past this pool, most likely thinking it too small to be worth a cast. But I gently took the fly off one of the guides of my rod, pulled out a little fly line, then made a series of false casts, before setting the proud little dry fly down with an almost grace.

A flash of silver and pink shot out from the dark, breaking the surface and greedily claimed the Humpy. She immediately regretted her decision and attempted to free herself of the fly as quickly as possible. But it was too late, I had her in the net!

I let out a series of giddy cries, and Mark and Jason walked back to help me with a photo of my first rainbow trout on dry fly! I almost felt a pang of guilt for deceiving her so easily and loosened my hand as she slipped away into the cold dark pool.

Around a slight bend there was a waterfall, which we heard and felt before we caught sight of it. Nowhere near the magnitude of the falls on the Guy Fawkes, but it carried a presence that had carved out its own mini escarpment. The water didn't come directly over the falls in a generally downstream direction but rather cut across a rock face from left to right.

It wasn't long before Jason brought to hand an almost clone of the trout I had just released. This one was destined for the smoker, so after a quick dispatch, Jason threaded his left pinky finger under the gills.

We fished that pool for a while longer, never really having much more interest but completely mesmerised by the gushing water, large ferns, and hanging moss from the deformed shrubbery on the crest of the escarpment.

The sky grew darker and a gust of wind gave a foreboding of imminent rain. Within minutes the rain set in – we would soon learn the unpredictability of the weather in this special part of the world.

Jason and I made a beeline for the hut but Mark, still having not caught a fish, donned a poncho from his backpack and continued upstream with his fly rod.

The rain soon passed, and as the sun bid its final farewell through a gap in the low dark clouds on the horizon, we traipsed across grass heavy with rain and glowing a vibrant straw colour in the golden evening light.

Back at the cabin, I took care of Jason's trout. Gutted whole with the gills removed. I grabbed the small galvanised iron smoker Mark and I had gone halves in purchasing at the tackle shop earlier, and took it outside. After placing the small spirits burner on the ground near an outdoor firepit, I filled it with methylated spirits, then took the wire racks out of the main box and laid down some foil before sprinkling in a generous sawdust mix of native timbers. Light flashed off the matchstick as I struck it against the box, then I cupped it in my hand to protect it from the mountain breeze and lowered it to the burner. Blue tongues of flame soon lapped up and over the edges of the burner. The smoker made some clinking noises as I lowered it over the flames, then I put a rack down and Jason's trout on top of it.

I looked up and almost startled as Mark emerged from the spiky brush, the hood of his poncho casting a dark shadow across his face. I took in the scene and noticed that he too had a nice fat rainbow in his hand. "Just in time!" I said.

He handed me the fish, and I had it gutted and lying next to the other fish within a minute.

Thin trails of blue and grey smoke meandered up from the top of the smoker as I placed the lid down, then the smoke mushroomed out and around the box. If there is a better smell than that of fish smoking, I don't want to know about it. I was suddenly agonisingly hungry.

The next twenty minutes were painfully slow as we waited by the fire pit, but when I lifted the lid of the smoker I was punched in the face by a cloud of smoke *and* the rich aroma of rendered fish fat. The wait had been worthwhile.

Sitting by the fire, we pulled the now-browned rainbow trout from the wire racks and onto plates, while a lonely currawong let out a few cawing sounds as the last of the daylight was stolen away by the night. We took forks and picked away at the flaky pink flesh as it slid off the bones.

We had to do more of this, I surmised. It was simple honest food that filled my soul and made me hungry for adventure.

Chapter 10 – The Styx

I awoke early to the patter of rain on the cabin roof. I had a feeling the sun had risen but there was no morning birdsong to be heard through the rain, and behind the curtains there was nothing but grey and rain.

The cabin itself was quiet and no one else was stirring yet, so I unzipped my sleeping bag and put some more firewood into the big iron fireplace.

The rain then eased temporarily, so I grabbed my fly rod and walked through the lush sodden grass that instantly made my pants stick to my calves, then down to the creek. It was flowing as beautifully as ever, the dark sheen of the water contrasting vividly with the lush greenery overhanging the banks. I pulled some line off the reel and made a skilful cast to the head of the pool. The fly set down gracefully and within seconds was devoured by a willing trout. I brought the perfect plate-sized hen rainbow trout to hand before removing the hook and sliding her gracefully back home. The lyrics from Van Morrison's song 'Days Like This' drifted through my mind and I knew exactly what he meant.

CHAPTER 10 – THE STYX

Back at the cabin, the renewed warmth was beginning to lift my spirits even further, so I filled the billy and set it to boil on a gas cooker. Digging through the Esky I found a small pack of sausages and decided that would be breakfast, so put them into a cast iron skillet on the other gas cooker.

Breakfast was almost ready when Mark, as graceful as a giant caterpillar, emerged from his feather-down chrysalis to start making a coffee with red eyes. Jason was the last to emerge but he was dressed and keen to get going once breakfast was finished.

The fog was lifting now to reveal a stunning blue sky. There wasn't a breath of wind. For once it was starting to feel like summer, despite still being around twenty degrees Celsius.

I propositioned the others, "Hey, let's go check out the hatchery and see if one of the guys there can give us some pointers for some new spots to fish."

So we piled into the ute and headed back along the dusty pot-holed road towards the hatchery.

The Dutton Hatchery sits right alongside Serpentine Creek with a labyrinth of knee-high rearing tanks under an open shaded structure. A visitors centre is surrounded by deciduous trees and large evergreen pines, the European influence easily spotted.

At the door to the visitors centre, a large ginger cat strolled up and rubbed through all our legs before demanding we pat it with its constant nudging and meowing. We indulged the cat and, after it seemed satiated, we opened the door and heard a little bell chime.

After a brief wait, a solid man in navy cargo shorts and a cotton drill work-shirt proudly displaying the New South Wales Red Waratah emblem emerged from a door at the back of the room. We paid a few dollars each for a tour and he took us up the steps. At the top of the landing, there was a room with a big white projector screen, some chairs, and a series of fish tanks around the walls.

The fish tanks contained a bit of everything, from Murray cod, Australian bass, brown trout, rainbow trout, and then a tank caught my eye: brook trout. But as I looked around the tank I couldn't see anything. I was pretty disappointed, as I'd only ever seen one brook trout before – when Jason, Tim and I had fished the freezing cold Thredbo River in the Australian Snowy Mountains in 2008 on the June long weekend, and a guy had walked upriver towards us holding a thumping good trout by the gills: a big hook-jawed buck brookie that weighed on his scales 2.4kg gutted. It wasn't until a few years later that it really set in just how big that was for an Australian brook trout.

We took our seats in the chairs and our tour guide / hatchery worker turned on a somewhat dated short video that covered the hatchery operations and process. Once that ended, we walked back out into the light and down the stairs. He handed us a zip-lock bag of pellets each and we set out to see how the place operated.

First stop was a large shed where the fish were hatched from ova over the winter months, before being placed into larger tanks.

CHAPTER 10 – THE STYX

Some fish never progressed beyond these tanks and instead got used as fingerling trout for fish stocking for the rivers, creeks and some lakes in the northern half of New South Wales.

Back outside and up the hill were a series of tennis court sized ponds with signs such as:

Brown Trout: 1 year
Brown Trout: 2 year
Rainbow Trout: 1 year
Rainbow Trout: 2 year

We took turns flicking handfuls of pellets into the ponds from the small wooden jetties and ogled at the large pink cheeks of the two-year-old trout.

The guide must have heard us talking about the size of them and told us to make sure we saved some pellets for the end of the tour.

Back down the hill we entered an open-air shade structure with concrete tanks, and saw some thumping big trout keeping up with a circular current swirling around inside them. We fed a few of these and he explained that a lot of them were broodstock that would likely be stocked into a few of the local trout dams.

Outside something caught my eye – there was a massive rainbow trout flopping around in some freshly cut grass clippings! I quickly picked it up and realised it was all of about 3-4kg of rainbow trout before sliding it back into a nearby tank and watched as the grass clippings dispersed across the surface of the water.

He informed us that this was the conclusion of the tour and we proceeded to the edge of the river, where purpose-built concrete pads and fencing had been installed to assist the hatchery operations.

I'd been hoarding a handful of my trout pellets and knew this was where he meant for us to use them. I launched a big handful across the creek and watched them scatter down, before the water erupted in a spectacular explosion of brown and rainbow trout. A few pellets escaped the greedy youngsters, though I watched them intently as they floated downstream over a weed bed. At the end of the weed bed was a small submerged log sitting in a clear patch of river bed.

The pellet drifted over the log and the log upheaved itself from the river bottom and put its maw around the insignificant brown pellet, before turning and coming to rest exactly where it had rested before.

We must have gasped because the hatchery worker gave a knowing laugh and explained that this particular trout was a bit of a pet.

I said, "You should name him Boris, Big Bad Boris."

We all had a laugh and it seemed like a good segway into asking about some fishing spots where we could find some brown trout.

He rattled off about a half-dozen streams between the hatchery and Dorrigo, and at the end mentioned the Styx River. I explained we were staying nearby and had only been catching rainbows. He nodded his head knowingly and told us about a spot back down

CHAPTER 10 – THE STYX

the road, where we could access the river down a forestry trail, and explained that the browns were much more prolific than rainbows there.

We thanked him for the tour and the fishing access spot, then headed back the way we came. After passing the cabins, we drove down a very 'scenic' dirt road lined with towering eucalyptus trees and stunning tree ferns, then saw a sign for the forestry road and turned the ute down over a series of contour banks.

The track was rough and a mix of rough rock and sticky dark dirt. As we came around a final bend in the track, the trees opened up and we found a spot to pull over where the river ran clear over freestone rocks below. It was stunning, weaving its way in and out of the towering white eucalypts, with ferns making up the bulk of the underbrush. It was a lot wider down here but each pool seemed different and unique.

I decided that, with a lot of extra vegetation down here, I didn't particularly want to be snagging my flies on every cast, so grabbed my spin rod instead.

The three of us then walked down to the river and took in the sounds of the current gushing over the rocks and the gentle whispering of the wind caressing the leaves of the ancient trees. The air smelt fresh, earthy and pure.

Jason and I had both tied on some little hard body lures, which we had used with great success on the browns on our first trip. The river was a bit wider here so I hopped across some rocks to the opposite bank and saw Jason lob his little lure about twenty metres upstream into the crystal-clear shallow water.

About halfway across the stream, there was a small fallen branch waving its talons like fingers out of the water, so I landed my little lure just to the left of it and as soon as it hit the water Jason set the hooks on a nice brown trout. I turned back to watch my own lure just in time to see a brown roll out from under the tall overhanging grass on the edge of the river and aggressively hit my lure.

This was one of those rare situations where we had a double hook up, and of course it merited the use of a high five. Mark took a quick picture and we released the fish with their vibrant brown and red spots back into the unspoiled river. They were small shadows for a while before disappearing completely under the cover of ripples.

The sky went dark and it started to rain. We had made our way up to a section of water I like to call the pocket water. Exercise ball sized rocks were scattered down the river like a giant's spilled bag of marbles, and the water hit and deflected all around them creating hundreds upon hundreds of perfect ambush spots for a feisty trout to hide. The layout and spacing also made it easy to hop from one side of the river to the other without even getting your feet wet.

A few more small browns came to hand, then the rain started coming down hard. I went to jump across the rocks again and slipped onto my arse. I doubled back and tried to push my way

CHAPTER 10 – THE STYX

through the scrub on the edges of the river but it was impossibly dense. Seeing as there weren't any big holes of water in sight, we decided to pull the pin and head back to the car.

Going back by the river was going to be hazardous, as the rocks we hopped up to get here were now as slippery as an oil slick, so we opted to cut back through the scrub.

This proved to be a mistake. I felt something itchy on the back of my neck so went to brush it off with my hand and my blood went cold when I felt the slug-like texture of a leech that had picked his new host.

As we battled on hard through the scrub, we had to keep picking off leeches in hoards and untangling lines caught in thorny bushes. Finally we pushed into the clearing, loaded our rods and gear away before we took turns doing slow-motion twirls while the others searched for any leeches trying to catch a free ride out of this place. We all had a few leeches hiding on us, in one place or the other, and I was glad to see them go.

Jason then climbed in the driver's seat and advised us, "Hang on, this thing isn't 4x4 and that road out is going to be steep and slippery."

I hadn't even considered that and, as he punched the accelerator up and around the first bend, I felt the rear of the vehicle loose traction and slide out, flicking dark mud up the sides of the ute.

"Do you think we'll get stuck?" I asked Jason.

"If we don't stop we will be fine," he answered, and true to his word he held his foot almost flat as we rounded corners and chugged up the steep straights. We would momentarily gain traction in a rocky section, but they seemed to be few and far between.

We finally came around a final corner and saw the dusty potholed road ahead. I would never complain about it again.

Chapter 11 – Along Came Sarah
January - April 2011

After our three nights away, we returned on New Years Eve, driving back into civilisation with all its pros of electricity and all its cons of no trout stream right in front of the house. I had no idea that the course of my life was going to change drastically over the next 30 days.

I was still working at my casual bookshop job, and was enjoying making just enough money to put fuel in my old Corolla, hang out with friends, travel to gigs with my band mates, and go chase trout on the Macdonald River whenever I felt like it.

I had made a new circle of friends, even met a couple of sweet girls my age, but for whatever reason things had never really worked out or felt right romantically. I prayed for God's help to find the right one!

Then my friend Matt was having his 18th birthday party in a local restaurant, and I saw a girl across the other side of the dimly lit upstairs room. She was wearing a black dress with white polka dots and had straight brunette hair that flowed down past her shoulders. I'd never seen this girl before and I'd been friends with Matt for a touch over two years.

Once the formality of the party was winding up with the cake and some photos, a small group of us left the restaurant and walked up the palm tree lined Peel Street to hit a few pubs.

This was a Monday night and I had to work the following day. I had also driven myself so it wasn't going to be a wild night. Still, to my delight, the mystery girl was trailing along after us. Except she was with what appeared to be her boyfriend and his twin brother.

At this point I was almost resigned to not ask any questions, but curiosity eventually got the better of me as I sat holding a glass of lemonade. I leaned across the table to my mate Pat and subtly nodded across to where the mystery girl was sipping a vibrant purple cocktail called a 'Ninja Turtle' and laughing with her boyfriend and his brother. "Who's that?" I asked Pat.

"That's Sarah, the triplet," Pat replied,

"Oh, so she has two sisters?" I asked.

"Nah, nah, that's her two brothers there," said Pat as he gestured across the room.

It took me a minute to process the situation with fresh eyes, then a good half an hour to muster up the courage to go and introduce myself, but ultimately decided to do it anyway as I told myself if I hadn't met her in two years of hanging around this group I was likely not going to run into her again.

To my surprise, she was really friendly and had an infectious laugh, and I knew something was different this time, as my stomach felt aflame. After that night, we all started hanging out pretty often as a group and I would always message Sarah to see if she was coming to hang out with us, and she would always show up.

One night, however, everyone else bailed at the last minute, and we were the only two people who showed up. I half-expected her to leave, since it was just me and no one else. But it turned out we actually had a fair bit in common. We shared the same sense of humour and a mutual disgust of trashy behaviour.

Then, a few days later, I was hanging out with Pat at a fast-food establishment. It was a hot summer night, with droves of moths and bugs hammering into the bright lights of the car park, when Pat turned to me and said, "Are you going to take Sarah out for Valentine's Day? We still have a few tables left at Bellapoque, I can hook you up with a spot." At the time Pat was waiting tables and manning the bar at a Mediterranean restaurant in town called Bellapoque – I'd never been there myself, as it was way too up-market for me.

But I quickly had a look at the calendar on my phone to see how I would be looking financially and noted that Valentine's Day fell on the day before I got paid, and at present I had less than $20 to my name. Somewhat embarrassed I told Pat about my situation, and he said, "don't worry about it, I'll chat to the boss when I book your table and tell him you will be in the following afternoon to fix up the bill, he will be cool with it."

I felt somewhere that he wouldn't be cool with it, but I was wrong.

Valentine's Day came around and I had just hopped out of the shower when I started experiencing that same nervousness I'd had almost twelve months before with my driver's test. I brushed the condensation off the bathroom mirror with a towel, and haphazardly flicked my hair to one side, then put on some nice black pants, a button-up white shirt, and some nice dress shoes. This also just so happened to be the clothes I wore to work at the bookshop, except for the uniform shirt, but it looked good enough.

Then I climbed in my yellow 1981 Toyota Corolla and started off across to the restaurant where I was meeting Sarah.

The heat in February in Australia can be intense, and this was one of those days. It was either exceptionally hot or I was getting even more nervous. I'm almost certain now it was the latter.

Sarah and I met outside the restaurant doorway, then Pat greeted us and escorted us to our table for two, right next to the fish tank built into the wall that separated the dining area from the bar.

Seeing as we were right next to the fishtank, I figured it was an appropriate time to ask if she'd ever been fishing before. "Yep, I went with Pop and hated it," she said.

I said, "Let me guess, you went when you were little and he told you to be quiet and stop running around so you don't scare the fish?"

"How did you know?" she replied.

So I explained that this is most people's introduction to fishing and half the reason they can't stand it once they grow up. "I can take you fishing and I promise you'll enjoy it," I said.

She seemed hesitant, like her pop might secretly be waiting to tell her to be quiet again when we got out there, but she begrudgingly agreed.

Sarah and I went on a few more dates and things were going really well. I didn't want to introduce myself to her parents as someone who only worked three or four days a week for only four or five hours at a time, so started asking around for full-time work. Nothing was really on offer.

Then one day, Pat's mum told me that she had heard they were hiring workers to make hot cross buns in preparation for Easter. I applied through a labour hire company and dropped off my CV.

I had only just got back out to my car and drove down the road for fifty metres when the phone rang. I pulled over on the verge and quickly answered it. "Can you please come back to our office, a position just opened and you can start tomorrow."

So for a few months, as well as working in the bookshop, I made hot cross buns for twelve-hours at a time! It was fast paced and mind-numbing work, but the smell was incredible.

Then Easter rolled around and the work dried up. Luckily, the labour hire place got me another gig unloading semi-trailers from 4am to 8am Monday to Friday. I did this for about a month – until their regular guy would be back on deck – living a routine of unloading trucks from 4am-8am, going home and sleeping until 10am, then showering and heading over at the bookshop for a 11am-3pm shift. I was so exhausted that I didn't even have the chance to go fishing or take Sarah yet. Something needed to change.

Finally, the stars aligned and I got another call from the labour hire company. "We passed on your CV to a local engineering company, and they would like to give you an interview. They only ever take on one or two people per year, and usually they put you onto their books after six months if they like you."

I landed the position and now had full-time hours at casual rates working from 6am-2:45pm Monday to Friday. These hours meant I still had time in the afternoon to go fishing if I wanted, so I started packing the fly rod and a spin rod in the car, along with a change of clothes. I still remember getting my first full paycheck, and believe me when I say I earned every cent of that money, grinding mineral build-up off spray bars from industrial washing machines with a grinder and a wire wheel. The typical jobs that usually get passed on to first-year apprentices.

Now, I had always dreamed of owning a nice fly rod. I'd even handled a few in shops around the snowies and Launceston. But I could never really fathom the price. But this paycheck was good and I didn't have any responsibilities in the world yet, so I treated myself.

When my allotted fifteen-minute 'smoko' break came, I found the number for a fly shop in Launceston, because I recalled having a chat to the owner and him mentioning going to high school

CHAPTER 11 – ALONG CAME SARAH

in Tamworth so figured we would have some common ground. I told him what I was after and what my budget was, and he recommended a four-weight, even made up a package for me with reel and some line. I gave him my debit card details over the phone, put the phone back in my pocket and went back to work.

I arrived home the following day to find an express post parcel on the end of my bed, the same place Mum used to put presents for my brother Mark and I on Christmas morning. I couldn't wait to try the rod out!

Then I remembered that, when driving out to Sarah's place for dinner with her parents, I always passed over a creek likely to be full of carp. So I had a shower to get rid of the caked-on layers of metal shavings and black dust that left an almost permanent metallic taste in the back of my throat, then drove to a bridge near their house.

By this stage the sun was getting low on the horizon and the wind was just strong enough to make the tall grass on the verge wave back and forth. Walking down to the bridge, I side-stepped a needle left near the guardrail and peered over the parapet into the brown shaded water below.

In the shadow of the bridge were some clumps of weed, and amongst those I could see some dark shapes and bright orange ones too. It looked like someone had just given up on their indoor fish tank and thrown their goldfish into the creek.

Before then, I had only caught one carp on fly, which was also the first fish I caught on fly. so fly selection wasn't my strong suit yet. Still, I stuck with what I knew and pulled a Scotch Poacher fly out of the box and tied it on. I pulled some line off the rod's slick little new reel and started on some false casts. The rod felt amazing! Especially after coming from the big heavy composite material entry level rod I had been using.

The fly hit the water near the school of aquarium escapees and sat on the surface. I remember being told to 'wet' wet flies before casting them so they sink straight away but it was hard from my elevated position on the bridge. I hadn't even considered what might happen if I actually hooked one of these fish and needed to land it, as the banks were pretty steep and overgrown, likely to be home to venomous snakes. So, from my elevated platform, I dunked the fly up and down until eventually it got water logged enough to start sinking, then I recast to a cool-looking black and orange carp.

He turned to look at the fly, then rolled on his side in refusal and dove down in the water column until he was gone.

I was just about to lift the fly from the water when I caught the sight of a pair of blubber lips inhaling the fly below, so paused momentarily before setting the hook and lifting into the weight of the fish.

The fish wasn't very big and didn't put up a fight, which I found somewhat surprising given how well that first carp had fought, although it was at least ten times the size of this fish.

I now had a couple of choices – risk lifting it vertically about four metres or so with the light leader, or find a way down off

CHAPTER 11 – ALONG CAME SARAH

the bridge. I decided to make my way to the western end of the bridge, where I hopped over the steel guard rail and bashed my way through shoulder-height grass, praying I wouldn't run into any brown snakes, all the while holding my rod above my head with pressure on the fish. The fish wasn't even fighting, just sitting on the surface with its head out of the water.

I was about to take another step before I realised there were no steps left to take – the tall grass was covering a three-foot drop off into the creek! I took a step back, grabbed my landing net, got down on my belly and scooped the docile fish into it.

When I returned the following day, there were no more aquarium school fish swimming around, so resigned myself to do some casting practice. I stood on the northern face of the bridge, facing downstream, and after checking no cars were coming I laid out the best cast I'd ever done up until that point. It wasn't the full fly line but there were only two loops of fly line left on the reel. I stripped the line, and a split second later my fingers were scorched from the line as it was torn from my grip. The backing knot disappeared out the ends of the guides, making a tink-tink-tink sound as it went.

With the sun already set, this fish was summoning up the power of a paranormal creature, spurred on by the growing darkness in its underwater realm. I doubted the rod would have the stopping power, but kept a low sideways angle on the fish and managed to turn the battle in my favour.

By now the world had descended into darkness, the water reflecting the silver-grey light of the moon. I climbed over the guard rail and got into a position where I might be able to land the fish. I found a spot, though it was still a good three-foot drop off to the water line.

The fish's head finally burst above the surface and I guided it gently but firmly to the place I had my waiting landing net. It went in about two thirds of the way before its head bottomed out in the base of the net and the water exploded like raw sodium in a bucket as I quickly yanked the net upwards.

A loud crack echoed back from under the abutments of the bridge and a group of swallows burst out of their mud houses in a flurry. The net slipped, so I reached down and grabbed a chunk of the net itself and fell backwards with the fish!

The fish was so heavy it had broken my good landing net. It was by far the biggest fish I'd ever landed on a fly rod, let alone a four-weight fly rod.

I was to enjoy these quick afternoon carp sessions immensely, though deep down I knew they couldn't replace the place in my heart that trout had come to occupy. I needed to get out onto a trout stream with my new rod!

Chapter 12 – Within an Hour
May 2011

It was late May and Mark and I were discussing a trip to finish off the trout season before it closed on the June long weekend. We were both pretty time-starved so didn't want to make the almost three-hour journey to Ebor, and the MacDonald hadn't fished well the past few times I'd been there.

Then I asked him, "Have you ever been to this creek I heard my Biology teacher mention?"

He said he hadn't, so I did some searching to find an access point and we came up with a plan.

The next weekend we made the fifty-minute or so drive from town to arrive at the place I had found online. Winter was starting to set in already and there were still patches of frost in the shadows of the gums where the rays of the sunrise hadn't reached yet.

I tied on a big size 12 Royal Wulff and put a nymph on a dropper about a foot below. This creek was really eye-catching with its clear flowing water over freestone rocks, the towering mountains of The Great Dividing Range standing firm beside it and casting shadows that plunged the whole valley into a pre-dawn light, until around mid-morning. Soon the birds were awake and declaring the day for themselves.

The first run right beside where we parked the car looked picture-perfect, something you'd expect to be in a fly fishing magazine, though we had no signs of fish yet, just a gut feeling. I did have the thought that maybe if there weren't any fish in that run there weren't any fish at all, it had looked too good.

Around the first bend we found a slower moving long pool that was bordered by rows of leaning and creaking casuarinas. The deepest part was hard up against the exposed root systems of these trees. Mark went upstream slightly, but I was determined to see if anything was hiding amongst the tree roots.

I was starting to get cold, though, as the sun still wasn't in the valley and my PVC waders were just not cutting it in the icy water. I got a decent cast up to the base of a tree and let it drift back towards me. I took my eyes off my dry for two seconds to look at my frozen fingers before I glanced back up and realised that the dry was gone.

I assumed it had most likely gotten water-logged as I didn't have any floatant, so I lifted the line to bring it back to hand to see if I could dry the fly off. As I did, the dark slow water came to life and in a boil of water at the surface I saw the flush pink cheeks of a rainbow like a signal mirror. The line went slack and I got mad at myself for missing the strike on that fish.

Later, we waded around a bend in the creek, where the sun was finally beginning to touch the frosty ground on the surrounding banks. The creek was beginning to narrow in this section and the trees were sparser. I caught a movement out of the corner of my eye and gazed at the source of it. A few seconds later, a small trout rose to the surface and scoffed something down like an unchaperoned child at a birthday party around the snack table.

Hoping that the fish shared the mentality of the greedy child at a party and would come back for a second, third or fourth helping, I crouched down and snuck into the casting range of the last set of ripples the fish had made, stripped some line off the reel, made a few back casts, and the fly landed about a metre to the left of the last known position of trout. I was already second-guessing the accuracy of the cast as the Royal Wulff drifted slowly towards me, but my worry was all for naught as the greedy little trout launched into the air like a great white on a fur seal! The fish was all of about twenty centimetres, but made up for the lack of length with the stunning strike visuals and aerobic performance.

The fish had water-logged the fly substantially and it wasn't floating at all afterward. I tried blowing on it a few times but it was too far gone. I pulled the fly up and bit the line off, and then things got hard. My hands were so numb from the cold and icy water that the dexterity had left my fingers. I sat trying to thread the tippet through the hook eye with hands that felt like thick oven mitts.

Finally, after much struggle, I got the line through the tiny eye but could barely muster up the strength to finish tying the knot. When the knot did come tight, at that exact moment I had the daunting realisation that I still had to tie my dropper nymph back on!

After what seemed like hours, but was probably only ten minutes, I was re-rigged and ready to go.

We came to a fast-moving section of water where the creek was narrower, faster and deeper as it stepped down through the whispering casuarinas. Mark got into a good position and soon had a nice rainbow trout to hand. I backed out and gave him a wide berth to let him finish working the water while I checked out the hole ahead.

Once I stepped out of the canopy of the casuarinas, the creek opened up wider and swept around ninety degrees to the right. A single tree stood just inside the water on the right-hand side and a kingfisher had found himself a perfect little perch from which to hunt. To the left there was a sheer rockface, growing lichen and moss. The water against that rockface was clear and deep, I couldn't see the bottom, only shadow, so got a feeling that if there was a big fish in this creek, he was going to be residing in this hole, and chances are I would be able to sight-cast him.

I took a few steps upstream to find a good position to start casting when I stopped dead.

At eleven o'clock there was a large straw-coloured shape gliding along beneath the surface. My heart began to race, this fish was huge! It had shoulders that would make Arnie blush. This was a fish of a lifetime for a creek like this and would be every bit of ten pounds.

CHAPTER 12 – WITHIN AN HOUR

My throat went dry. The fish was still powering towards me. I quickly unhooked the fly from the rod and attempted a very finesse cast somewhere on the big brute's collision course. The fish was closing in at a rate of knots. But, as soon as I went to move my rod hand, the fish about-faced, and left a puff of sediment in the layer of organic matter sticking to the bottom of the pool.

It was only after the fish had bolted that I realised what had happened. It wasn't a trout, it was a carp. A big smelly, invasive, bottom feeding carp. Hadn't I come all this way to get away from chasing these in town? I was just about to move on when another pale shape glided towards me on the same trajectory as the previous fish. Right next to this one appeared two duplicates on his flanks. The three of them got to the patch of water where the sediment was stirred up from the previous fish, then quickly turned back to the safety and security of the deeper water.

I turned back and told Mark what I had seen as he wandered up behind me. He seemed just as surprised as I was by the carp being here, although it shouldn't have really been a surprise as they were present downstream of this spot and in massive numbers in the river into which this creek fed.

Around the corner of the big hole, there was a section that looked like it was used as a crossing for farm vehicles. I made a cast and the fly line laid down straight before drifting back down across the shallow free stone bottom. The dry disappeared and I first thought that perhaps it had become snagged on a rock in the shallows, but having learnt from my previous encounter I set the hook.

Fish leapt from the water several times in a display of silver and navy against the sun rising above the range, then made a rush downstream to the big hole where the carp were swimming. I got my net ready and, while the fish started to fatigue, glanced back upstream.

Mark had laid out a beautiful cast in pretty much the same spot. I was about to yell out that he was wasting his time, but bit my tongue because at that exact moment he lifted his rod. The line made that slurp noise any fly fisher knows and loves – the sound of the line ripping off the surface tension with the weight of a fish underneath.

So I quickly netted my fish and hurried to where Mark was playing his catch out. I assisted him and landed his fish. We took some photos of the pigeon pair of fish, then let them go.

For the next stretch of creek, we hooked a fish in every single hole. Mind you, we didn't land all of them. This was unfortunately the case as I cast in between a large fallen gum laying across the creek and a blackberry bush. A solid rainbow in the fifty plus centimetre bracket rolled out from under the shadow of the log and inhaled the nymph. I set the hook and the fish made a series of acrobatic displays before finally, in a frantic jump out of the water, it managed to get some of the leader around the thorns of the overhanging blackberry and disappeared back into the deep hole beneath the log.

CHAPTER 12 – WITHIN AN HOUR

Ultimately, the fishing was exceptional, with hungry rainbows in every other hole we cast into. We eventually came to a section of the creek where the river ran deep and fast between two large rocks.

Mark tied on a bead head nymph and worked deep through the current and extracted a fantastic fish.

The sun was getting high now and the whole valley was kissed with morning sun from an unblemished blue sky. Up the hill on our right, the road cut through the hillside, so by now it would be quicker to climb up to it and walk back along the road then traverse painstakingly back through the creek the way we had come.

I was determined to catch one more fish before calling it a day. The next little run was deep on one side under the roots of the casuarinas and shallow on the left where it ran over river rock. There was a driftwood log submerged, running from the top to bottom of the pool, and from where I was standing I could see enough shadows under the log to know it was a perfect trout habitat.

The nymph set down with a subtle 'plop' at the head of the pool and, seconds later, I saw a flash from under the log, I struck, lifting the rod, and as I did a tiny baby trout was hurled backwards from its hole and landed next to me in the water. The overzealous strike was no match for the little fish. I was laughing like mad and, after explaining to Mark what had happened, thought a fish that small deserved a photo – which is when Mark and I noticed something was wrong. There was no trout on the end of the line, but there was a small fish that had nailed a nymph, except it had colours similar to a Murray cod.

I thought for a second it might be a Murray cod fingerling but something was different. I reached into my bag and found a fisheries guide, which is where I immediately saw this was a river blackfish! I had absolutely no idea they lived around here, but here was one in my hand.

I carefully unhooked the poor little guy, slid him back into the water and he powered upstream before rolling back under the safety of his log. It may have been a tiny fish but it left me feeling electrified, and brought up the total number of species caught on fly for me.

We turned to face the road, climbed up the hill, and walked back to the car. On the walk back, I thought the creek would be the perfect place to bring Sarah.

But with the season closing soon, it would have to wait until at least the October long weekend.

Chapter 13 – The Trout Farm
Winter 2011

Sitting in the hills above Nundle is a hidden gem: Hanging Rock. Forest and farms abound. There are also two decent-sized dams that are regularly stocked with trout, named the Sheba Dams.

But down a gravel road to the south of these dams, past a few cattle grids and bovine pedestrians, is a family owned and run trout farm. The entrance to the farm takes you from the open fields above and winds you down into a different world of lush green ferns and mighty eucalypts.

One miserable winter day, complete with spatterings of rain and a greyed-out sky, I decided to become a man on a mission: to get Sarah to catch a trout with relative ease – mainly to show her it was a fun and not an impossible task, before testing her skills in the wild on some more pressured fish, where the immediate gratification might not be as easily achieved.

We rounded the final bend in the driveway to the farm gate building and, to our right, sat the designated fishing dam. The water was a murky combination of green, grey and blue, but contrasted well with the smooth white bark of eucalypts beyond.

Clusters of ferns and sprawling tussock grass filled the pockets of the hillside.

We came prepared with raincoats, and the rain was indeed soon hammering down. With muddy feet, we approached the front door of the building – a building where I had my first ever paid job. When I was seventeen, I had worked here for three days with my friend Tim leading up to the Easter long weekend.

It had involved early morning starts and long days consisting of taking fish from the ponds, taking them to the processing room, and gutting or filleting as many as possible. By the end of our third day, Tim and I had become trout gutting champions, often having small races to see who could do one the fastest. It was here that the owner Russell showed Tim and I a cool trick from the gut pile of our fish. He carefully removed the hearts and placed them together on the stainless-steel bench. Right before our eyes, the hearts started to beat in unison.

I thoroughly enjoyed my time working there and especially loved the smell that wafted through the processing room each time the door to the smokehouse was opened.

It was that same smell of wood smoke and rendering trout fat that graced my nostrils as I again pushed open the door with Sarah, seeking respite from the rain. The warmth of the room was like a wave and for an instant I didn't want to go back out – until Russell told me that the ova were beginning to hatch down in the hatchery and offered us a tour.

CHAPTER 13 – THE TROUT FARM

We accepted the offer and went with him down the hill through the lush native forest before arriving at the hatching shed. Small narrow tables had been set up to imitate the shallow waters of the preferred egg locations of a trout stream, and were full of bright orange balls. In a few of the table tanks, minute brown sticks now floated around amongst the blaze orange orbs. These sticks were of course the freshly hatched trout, which had only just emerged from their eggs hours before we had arrived.

We watched them ebb and flow up and down in the gentle tank currents for a while, it was almost hypnotic. It was also mesmerising to think about the fairly rapid transformation the small sticks would make over the next twelve to eighteen months, growing into catchable and edible trout.

With that thought we made our way back up the hill, hired a rod for Sarah (quarantine reasons, to protect their trout), grabbed a tray to put fish in and a landing net, then walked the short distance up to the dam.

The rain was starting to settle in now and Sarah pulled the hood of her raincoat over her hair and tightened the drawstrings around her face. When we got to the dam, I saw a guy dressed in top-to-bottom yellow rain gear slowly sliding down the hill towards the water's edge, unable to maintain his grip in the sticky red clay. I had a bit of a chuckle and hoped I would not share a similar fate.

When I next glanced up, he had slid so far that his gumboots were just inside the edge of the water.

After a comical few minutes of the mystery yellow guy shouting out, I realised he sounded familiar. It was only when I saw another man close by, unable to contain his laughter, that I realised they were friends of mine. I got talking to them and they told me they had been there for the past three weekends in a row trying to catch their first fish, without any success.

Of course doubt then flooded my mind. Had I made a bad decision bringing Sarah here to this wet, cold, and now muddy place?

The voice of reason (or stubborn denial) prevailed and I told Sarah the basics. The farm had provided us with a small jighead and some small scented soft plastics. I took one from the packet and lined it up on the jighead before pushing it through and making sure it wasn't bent or deformed on the hook.

Under some careful instruction, I got Sarah to cast to the opposite bank from us, let it sink, give it a few cranks up with the rod tip before winding in the slack and repeating the process. This action was supposed to imitate a small crayfish scurrying up off the bottom.

After about ten minutes, the guys I knew left fishless, and we were already starting to feel the cold. I really felt like fishing myself, but had a job to do – I had to get Sarah to catch a fish. It was the number one priority.

Then it happened. I heard the unmistakable sound of the drag on a spinning reel tick over and looked to see the rod Sarah was using under a full load, with an energetic trout on the other end.

CHAPTER 13 – THE TROUT FARM

After a brief tussle, I grabbed the net and carefully got into a position on some grass, trying to avoid placing my feet in the clay soil of the dam that might have me falling in. I didn't want to be like my unfortunate friend unable to stop myself sliding into the water.

My plan worked and I triumphantly scooped the fish into the net. I gave it a quick dong over the head with a provided stick and placed it into the plastic tub that the trout farm had provided. But, much to Sarah's trauma, the fish began to flop in the container and a further blow was needed.

I gave Sarah the option to call it a day or keep fishing. She decided the rain was too uncomfortable now, so we went down to the farm building to get the fish processed and weighed – the caught fish were sold by weight once caught. It was an effortless transaction, we handed them the container, they brought back a gutted and packaged trout to take home.

We said our goodbyes and climbed back into the ute. The rain was now coming down relentlessly and the road was turning to slush. Coming around a corner, there was a cattle grid across the road. I tapped the brakes lightly to reduce my speed, but before I knew it, the ute was sliding sideways, then backwards, and we were on the wrong side of the road, facing back the direction we had just come. I felt like nothing I could have done differently could have avoided what happened. Yet at the same time I was relieved that we hadn't fallen off the edge of the road and down an embankment!

Descending from the clouds of Hanging Rock, passing through the town of Nundle, the rain started to ease up. We made it down to the back end of Chaffey Dam at Bowling Alley point, with Sarah enjoying some mini M&M's from a large packet. Just after we crossed the bridge, I spotted a fox sitting in a dirt track just off the bridge, trying to soak some warmth from the intermittent sun rays passing through the clouds.

I pulled the ute over and pointed to the fox to show Sarah, then before maturity kicked in, I was accelerating towards my unintended prey like a coursing dog! The distance between us was closing rapidly and the fox was too stunned to run, frozen in fear at what he was seeing, just on the other side of a puddle.

The front end of the ute plunged into the puddle and bottomed out with a thud. Red clay puddle-water sprayed wildly in the air outside, while simultaneously inside a confetti gun of rainbow mini M&M's showered down around us. Once the self-imposed storm had passed, and the wipers had pushed the last of the remaining mud off the windscreen, we saw the bobbing white tip of the fox's tail disappear into the long grass.

"Why did you chase it?" Sarah said in a somewhat scared but slightly amused tone.

I just shrugged, reached down into the centre console, grabbed a handful of the mini M&M's and shoved them in my mouth.

Four years later when I sold the ute, I found a single green mini M&M under the seat.

Chapter 14 – Into The Trees

October 2011

The chill of winter was still fresh in the spring air when the October long weekend and the new trout season came around. Sarah and I were heading back to what was to become my favourite trout stream. I rigged up my best 1-3kg spin rod for her and stashed a small box of spinners and lures into my fishing bag, which was now resting between the passenger seat and centre console as we bounced up the gravel road to the access point.

The road started to get closer to the creek as we wound our way up the valley, and as the towering mountains grew closer together the road was squeezed into a single car width track, winding its way through ancient gum trees and scrubby undergrowth.

The access spot was empty and it didn't look like any cars had parked there for a while, which hopefully meant we would be the first to fish this beat that season.

The river itself was running clear and cold as I took my first step into the water to cross to the less overgrown side. This was only Sarah's second time fishing and her first time to test her newly acquired skills on some wild fish. I tied her on a small hardbody lure in a rainbow trout pattern, the same one I had used on my first trip to Ebor with Jason, then explained how to cast upstream into the centre of the creek and to start winding it back in immediately.

She flipped the bail arm over, swung the rod back and launched that little lure into the highest point of the closest casuarina tree, where it got stuck.

"This is going to be a long, expensive day," I thought to myself.

With some careful flicks I was able to dislodge it and send it hurtling back towards us.

I told Sarah to go a little easier on the next cast.

She nodded, flicked the rod back and, this time, the lure hit the opposite bank and got stuck in some grass.

I couldn't coax it out this time, and didn't want to spook all the fish by wading through to retrieve it. So I got Sarah to stay with the rod while I cast a dropper rig with a caddis and bead head nymph up to the head of the pool by a lone boulder in the centre of the creek.

I watched the caddis intently as it drifted back past the boulder and, as soon as it cleared the boulder, it vanished from sight. I thought for a split second that the nymph might have gotten stuck on the rock, but decided to chance the strike anyways.

The decision paid off and I was met with the reverberating rhythm of a trout through the grip of the four-weight. It was a pretty little trout, with vibrant violet cheeks and almost silver colouring across the body with a heavy coating of freckles on top. I gently removed the nymph from the corner of its mouth and slid it back into the icy clear water. After two tail flicks, she vanished into the labyrinth of freestones.

Something changed in Sarah after I caught that fish. I'm not sure if it was built-in rivalry from being a triplet, or that it had just become something that she needed to do, but she was going to fish.

After I unsnagged the lure from the grass and we walked up to the start of the next pool, the pool where I had had my first encounter with a trout in this creek, Sarah had her game face on. She landed the little lure in pretty much the same spot I had landed a fly on my previous outing, right at the base of some overhanging Casuarina roots, and she had no sooner flipped the bail arm back and wound the rod a couple of times when I heard the first little click click sound of the drag.

The water transformed itself from still and dark to erupting and white. Sarah remained calm and I effortlessly cornered the trout and scooped it into the net. This fish was at least ten centimetres bigger than mine, but I wasn't jealous. Well, maybe a little, but just shallow jealousy. Deep down I was happier seeing her catch this fish than I was my own.

We made our way upstream fishing all of the usual haunts that Mark and I had discovered before the season closed. The trout were home in some of them and gone in others, but we also managed to find some in places where they hadn't been before.

We came out at the pool we now referred to as 'The Carp Pool' and true to its name a half dozen carp were working a beat along the pool's perimeter. I tied on some small wet flies I had been using in the rivers and lakes for carp, but could not even so much as get an inclination of interest from these lock-jawed fish. Only after I changed flies back to the dropper rig, did I manage to pull a nice rainbow from the head of the pool. It was so interesting to see how the two species could cohabitate.

Still, I felt the need to try and remove them one day.

The afternoon was getting away now and the sun had started to dip behind the mountain to the west, which cast a large shadow across the valley floor and instantly dragged the temperature down with it. The fish were starting to rise, eager to take the caddis over the nymph, so I cut the nymph off and stashed it back in the fly box.

For the next forty-five minutes the fishing was incredible, we pulled a trout from every pool right up to the point where we hit the sharp bend in the river, just where the road went past in an S-bend above. We had both been so distracted by the quality of the fishing that we now came to the realisation that it was so dark we could only just make each other out from five metres away.

Without a torch, it was too dark to make our way back via the creek, so I made the call to scramble up the near vertical hillside to the S-bend so we could walk back along the road.

The hill was a killer and we were soon both gasping for air and barely halfway up. We pushed through some small bushes, growing determined to get to the road before it was impossible to see anything at all.

CHAPTER 14 – INTO THE TREES

Sarah brushed her arm as we emerged from the scrub and onto the road and let out a disapproving sigh. "You walked me through sticky beaks!" she exclaimed.

I used the torch on my phone and scanned over her, the long sleeve jersey she was wearing now had a look not too dissimilar to an echidna. It was at this moment that I realised my own error, I took my hat off to find it completely covered also.

The moon was lightly illuminating the valley now with the sound of crickets chirping away beneath the grass. The gravel road looked bioluminescent as it guided our way back, while the wind sent us tendrils of fresh water and eucalyptus in a warm spring breeze.

The night was pleasant but there was a definite tension in the air between us now as I watched Sarah in her futile attempt to make her jersey sticky beak free.

Back at the car, I took to picking off as many as I could, but it seemed to be as efficient as draining the ocean using a bucket.

I looked Sarah in the eyes, and while I could see the annoyance at the burs written plainly, there was a spark behind it that told me she would do it again next weekend if I but asked the question.

Chapter 15 – Dorrigo Gentlemens Gathering

July - December 2012

It was a winter's day in mid-July by the turquoise water of the Swansea channel. The air was crisp, cold and laden with the briny smell of the ocean, while the sun battered its way around the patchy silver cloud cover.

Myself, and Mark had travelled from Tamworth, to meet up with a bunch of strangers we had met on the internet, which ran counter to any advice we had received from our parents and teachers during our school years.

We had come here to catch Australian salmon on fly rods, which despite the name have no relation to the salmonid species. The only things they really have in common are their willingness to eat flies, albeit Surf Candies and Clouser Minnows instead of traditional wet flies and streamers. However, the Australian salmon is built for speed. A silver and green spotted torpedo with a large powerful forked tail.

It was while Michael 'Youngy – The Non-Thinking Man's Fly Fisher' Young and I were simultaneously hooked up to salmon and doing our best to stop them from taking all our line and backing from his flat decked fibreglass boat, that he mentioned

CHAPTER 15 – DORRIGO GENTLEMENS GATHERING

that himself and a few other guys often met at Dorrigo each year to chase trout and beers for a weekend in early December. It wasn't his place to invite me, but he would put in a good word with the secret societies event organiser.

A few months later, my brother Mark and I received our invitations via text message and confirmed our attendance. The gathering was kicking off on the Friday, but I was unable to get out of work. Thankfully we always finished at midday on Fridays, which meant I would arrive in Dorrigo by around 3.30pm that afternoon.

Time was standing still, and the metal grinding I was doing was gruelling and monotonous. I kept glancing up at a stationary clock on the workshop wall and could have sworn that the clock was broken.

I checked back at the clock regularly and, when the hands had failed to move for the third time, I put the grinder down and went and spoke to the foreman. "What are my chances of getting out of here early?" I asked diplomatically.

"If you can finish the one you are on, you can finish up for the day and work back the forty-five minutes on Monday afternoon," was the reply I got as I eagerly turned back to finish grinding.

Sparks flew everywhere as I applied extra effort for the next five minutes. Once the gleaming metal object was shining back with glossy edges, I knew I was done. I locked my toolbox, washed the caked layers of grinding dust off of my arms, hands, face, and shot the foreman a goodbye wave through his office window while he made a phone call, and bolted for my packed and waiting ute in the car park outside.

About half way to Dorrigo, I pulled over to get changed out of my work gear and into fishing gear before I hit the high country, just in case I found a stream I couldn't drive past. A few minutes down the road, the sky began to darken and a few minutes after that the sky opened up with steady constant rain.

As I drove past Ebor, I spotted a few of the guys from the salmon fishing trip earlier in the year exiting the local cafe, so I did a U-turn to pull over and see how everything was going.

"We got onto a few this morning down at the Styx," said the man who had organised the event, "but then this rain came over so we have been up here trying to get away from it."

A decision was made and we all jumped back on the B78 and made our way to the Dorrigo Pub, which was to be our home for the next three days.

The rain was relentless in its assault on our foolishly planned weekend. "Should have been here yesterday," said the lady running the bar, which doubled as the accommodation reception area. "Beautiful blue skies and no wind all week until today."

CHAPTER 15 – DORRIGO GENTLEMENS GATHERING

Comments like that would go on to become recurring dreams on trips I would make for years to come. Nightmares are dreams too.

I headed up for the room I had been assigned that I would be sharing with Mark. The room was surprisingly spacious with high ceilings up on the second storey of the pub, with a door that meant you could step right out onto the wrap-around verandah that had views across the busiest intersection in town, which compared to city living was not very busy at all.

There was a small desk with good lighting around it, just next to the bathroom with red timber framing around a mirror, presumably for people to sit in front of and make themselves look presentable. I had a better use for it as I pulled a shoebox out of my duffle bag and placed my fly tying vise at the table, grabbed some elk hair, hackle, thread, dubbing and head cement and got to work on making some flies that would be more than presentable to the local trout.

I had just finished tying my third fly for the night when I heard a light tapping on the window that overlooked the town, I could see a large silhouette framed in the window behind the lacey white curtains. I pulled the curtain back and saw Youngy with his face pressed against the glass making it fog up. Neither of us could keep a straight face and burst out laughing.

Mark had also arrived and was letting himself into the room right while this all unfolded and seemed a little bit confused as to what was going on, but was disarmed once he saw us laughing.

We made our way downstairs to the bistro area and discussed the next day's plans over a rump steak with Diane sauce and a couple of schooners.

We would break off into groups of two or three and cover a few different streams between Dorrigo and Ebor. Mark and I decided to buddy up the following morning and hit a small rainforest creek that we knew held brown trout.

The rain never stopped through the night and continued into the morning. I was more than happy to roll back over and get a sleep in after a big week at work. Around mid-morning, or gentlemen's hours as it was to become known, was a much more fitting time to start the day for this gathering. The lure of the bakery across the street was too hard to resist, so I donned my jacket and made a dash across the wide country street to grab a meat pie, which proved to be the perfect equaliser to cold and wet weather. Then it was time to make our way to the stream.

As soon as Mark and I arrived at the stream, we came up with a game plan to hike as far downstream as possible, then fish our way back. We left the fog-covered road behind and wove our way through a maze of vines, ferns and eucalypts. The river was flowing hard and we could hear the water cascading over the top of the waterfall and into the large pool behind.

Each step in the undergrowth of the forest let out an earthy smell of fresh dirt and wet eucalyptus. It felt untouched down here, and despite the surrounding farmland this valley was very much untouched Gondwana rainforest.

CHAPTER 15 – DORRIGO GENTLEMENS GATHERING

It was hard to comprehend that trout were actually introduced to this system, or that they had adapted to the cool clear water and rainforest surrounds. It was as if this was where they had always been.

I pushed aside some vines and got a glimpse of the stream running through the fern-lined banks, right as some large water droplets alighted from laden leaves high above and crashed on and around me, echoing through the inside of my rain hood. The stream itself was clear over the rocks below, in the shallows, but became tannin-stained in the deeper runs of pools.

As we soon discovered, there was absolutely no room to make a back cast, without getting hung up on the surrounding rainforest and precariously hanging vines. Bow and arrow casts and roll casts soon became the necessity for the day, and after a few teething issues with hooksets, the first small browns began to come to hand.

They were a far cry from legal size but were proving to be more of an antidote to the foul weather than the warm meat pie from the local bakery. Our progress back upstream through the thick vegetation was slow going, and our hands were going numb with the cold and wet.

We came to the base of a large waterfall flowing over dark rock, which vibrantly contrasted with the smooth white eucalypts that formed a sentry perimeter of the hole below, their outstretched hands shading the pool below.

I always found these larger holes more difficult to catch fish in, I don't know if it's the fact they get more angler pressure or there is just more slower moving water to cover as opposed to the shallower faster runs on the creek that I love fishing so much. Still, the next hour went by with Mark and I making cast after cast at the base of the falls, and after we both had some near misses with non-committal brown trout, we turned around and began the climb back up the hill.

We hadn't been paying attention to much else bar the fish and water, but the hike out was something else. A combination of summer heat and rainfall had created an almost liquid atmosphere in the air, through which we gasped, hanging onto vines, struggling through the undergrowth.

The sound of crashing water was, however, soon replaced by the gentle flowing of the water in the creek ahead. The sky had grown dark, late in the afternoon, and now the caddis were beginning to hatch. We both tied on new flies and, in the next pool we fished Mark enticed a nice brown trout to scoff the caddis as it skated down towards us.

The rain started to come down heavier as the trout distorted the surface of the pool, its every jump shattering the glass into white shards in amongst the bombardment of rain drops from the sky above.

I quickly jumped off the creek bed into tannin water below, my outstretched hand holding a landing net, but my feet hit the slimy surface of the flat rock below and I momentarily lost balance, until

CHAPTER 15 – DORRIGO GENTLEMENS GATHERING

the grip on my wading boots did what it was designed to do. I scooped into the net what would be the biggest fish for the day, a stocky little brown trout with large sparsely placed black spots.

But now the rain was bucketing down, and I didn't want to wreck my good camera, so I got some video on my action camera before Mark released the fish.

By then the sky had grown even darker, which was both a combination of the building storm and the disappearance of the sun in the late afternoon. So we both pulled our rain hoods down firm and made the dash through the last of the rainforest scrub to the car. When we got back to the pub we went straight upstairs to our room, changed into dry clothes and went back down into the bistro section of the pub to order food.

The rest of the gentlemen were already ordering, and behind them was a huge group of motorcyclists. The section of the waterfall way between Dorrigo and Bellingen is a very popular riding location, with winding bends down The Great Dividing Range through ancient Gondwana rainforest.

But as Mark and I took our place in the line behind the last of the riders, I looked at the sign above the serving counter:

Kitchen Closes at 8pm

I looked at my watch, 7:15pm – for once we weren't back late.

The line moved at a snail's pace due to the sheer volume of people ordering, and when we were halfway I glanced over to see Youngy tormenting us while he chewed into his perfectly cooked steak.

I hadn't even realised how hungry I was until then. It also dawned on me that I hadn't eaten anything since breakfast. There were only two riders left in front of us now and we still had fifteen minutes until the kitchen closed. They placed their order, about-turned and walked to their large group, and Mark and I stepped forward to the counter.

"Are you with the riding group?" the lady behind the counter asked.

"No, we are with the fly fishing group," I replied.

"Sorry kitchens closed, we close at 8pm," was the short reply.

"What are we supposed to do for food then, since we're staying here?"

She turned away and said, "try the pizza shop across the road, you are welcome to take it back to your rooms."

I turned to look at Mark and thought we'd better run over there before *they* stop serving for the night too.

By this point, I noticed that the rest of the gathering were cleaning off their plates and beginning to head back upstairs anyways. So we made a dash across the wide-open street. My nostrils were soon hit with the smell of a wood fire, melting cheese and rendering animal fat. We ordered a pizza each and, after a very brief wait, we were dashing back across the road and up the stairs, slightly damp pizza boxes in hand.

The rain had really settled in now and was just constantly heavy. The gentlemen had all gathered out on the top verandah of the

CHAPTER 15 – DORRIGO GENTLEMENS GATHERING

pub and were enjoying some beers, whiskeys, salami, cheese and other small goods.

I pulled up a seat with my back to the wall so I could watch the rain pommel down amongst the glow of white and amber street lighting on the town centre below. I took that first bite of pizza and was somewhat glad the pub didn't serve us. The perfectly cooked dough, melted cheese and crispy pepperoni reset everything right in the world.

Not long after I finished my pizza, someone emerged from their room with a fly rod in hand. "Check out my new eight-weight I bought for saltwater fly fishing!" that someone announced. "Let's have a casting competition!"

With the amount of beers and whiskeys consumed, of course no one saw the flaws in the proposition of having a casting contest on the 2nd floor balcony of a pub overlooking the two main streets of Dorrigo.

Before we knew it, we were all lined up along the handrail overlooking the main street and intersection waiting for our turn to cast the rod. The rain was bucketing down, so thankfully the streets were empty of unsuspecting pedestrians. Someone managed to slap a loop into a street sign and we all made a collective 'ooof' sound as the metallic sound echoed along the street. The next person stepped forward, grabbed the rod and started putting some line out. At that point, a 4x4 police ute rounded the corner, so he let the line flop to the ground as we slowly backed away from the railing.

I thought the fun was well and truly over, but the police never saw the fly line reaching from the verandah to the street. They didn't even slow down as they motored out of town. Despite getting away with it, everyone sort of seemed to agree that we should perhaps act like adults and step away from the edge.

A group of us including myself, Youngy, Mark and a few others instead sat around an outdoor table exchanging photos of fish we had caught over the weekend so far.

Youngy showed me a photo of him holding a solid one to two pound brook trout that he had caught a few days prior on his homemade one-weight glass rod. I could see from the subsequent photos that the stream was very narrow, so narrow in fact that most of it was obscured by overhanging grass and all but impossible to cast a fly in.

I was becoming electrified at the possibility of catching my first ever brook trout, especially since they weren't known to even exist this far north in Australia. Youngy walked me through how to get to the spot and, when he said there were only brook trout present in the creek, I couldn't have been more excited for the next day to come.

Chapter 16 – Trifecta

After a very restless night thinking about catching a brook trout, the sun broke the horizon and I rolled out of bed, packed up my bags, walked them down to my ute, then headed to the front desk to pay my account.

Mark had already left early to get back in time for prior commitments, so I decided to head out with one of Youngy's mates who went by the name Erro.

We had the single-minded thought of finding browns, so we tried driving down a few new roads to look at new water and found the access way too difficult. We ended up back on the all too familiar waterfall way and started driving towards Ebor in our separate vehicles. Every stream we drove over was in flood, each one a couple of feet higher than the banks and spewing chocolate milk downstream with debris.

I knew it had been a wet weekend but I hadn't given much thought to how much rain the area had gotten since we all arrived. I now realised it had been a lot. There was one final creek I knew held browns along this stretch of road and I prayed that it wouldn't be in flood.

I turned the corner and saw it was up a little higher than normal, maybe half a foot, but still running clear! Our cars pulled over on the narrow verge in unison, before we went through the almost sacred ritual of rigging up fly rods, donning a jacket and setting off upstream.

Erro hadn't fished this particular stream before so I shared what little rudimentary knowledge I had of those particular fish. "Last time I fished here, there always seemed to be a trout hanging right at the base of the pool, just above the rapids from the pool below which made them easy to spook, and once that first fish swam upstream it was game over for any chance of another fish from that hole" I explained.

Erro gave a nod of acknowledgement and placed a cast right where I had explained, but the line must have landed on the water right above a fish because bow waves soon shot right up the centre of the pool.

This wasn't going to be easy at all, and we had similar situations unfold at almost every hole.

Then there was a slight incident wherein which a small #16 nymph landed in the back of one of our heads and had to be removed!

Still, we fished up quite a way and discussed what we did for work, what type of fishing we liked best. Erro was used to fishing the world class fishery of the Western Lakes of Tasmania, which is a proper 'hunting' fishery. Each fish has to be spotted and a stalk placed to get an eat, blind casting out there on those big sparse alpine lakes just doesn't cut it.

Then the stream started to narrow right up and flow underneath the arms of outstretched trees making sections near impossible to get a cast under. Erro had to get back home so we said our goodbyes and, as he walked back to his car, I fished onwards into the drizzly rain.

After I came around a slight bend in the creek, a small opening in the scrub revealed a bathtub-sized pool of water between two sets of rapids. I was lost in a bit of trance, watching the water trickle over the free stones in the bottom of the creek, when I spotted something that didn't quite look right – there was a pale shape two thirds of the way to the opposite bank. I watched it move across a few rocks and, as it sipped a bug from the surface, it confirmed my suspicion.

I gently released the fly from the hook holder on my rod and gently pulled some line off the reel as I crouched down into the saturated green grass and leaf litter. The strong smell of crushed wet eucalypt and damp earth blazed through my nostrils as I took a breath to prepare to make a very accurate cast into the cavernous hole of scrub above the creek.

After one quick loading back cast, I let the line slip from my fingers and loop out across the grass, hoping the small caddis dry would find its target at the top of the pool. The loop rolled out straight and instead of falling gracefully onto the surface of the water it stayed outstretched in the air above. The caddis fly stuck in a branch above.

This was the best opportunity I'd had all day on a fish, and I'd blown it! The worst part was this was probably the last fishable pool in the whole upstream section of the creek. I pulled on the line to test how stuck it was, and the branch swayed towards me slowly before receding as I let the pressure go.

I was going to have to quickly break the fly off, hopefully without spooking the fish away. I applied straight pressure down the line and, to my shock, the fly let go and came hurtling back to my side of the creek – I would have a chance at redemption!

My heart started beating faster as I crawled closer to try and get a bow and arrow cast into the hole. I gripped the fly between my thumb and index finger, bent the rod over and released my arrow.

The fly landed right at the head of the pool and I watched it float straight past the resting fish.

I repeated this three more times with no interest from the fish, and started to think that I had spooked the fish while un-snagging my fly, but he had very limited options on where to go so had just bunkered down where he was.

This time, however, the fly landed down with a soft plop. The fish twitched and its body language changed, and turned towards the slowly drifting dry. He glided to intercept the fly's downstream trajectory and rose to enact his perceived ambush.

He sipped the fly down and, a few short seconds later, he would learn that this was not a game of him becoming an ambush preda-

CHAPTER 16 – TRIFECTA

tor, but rather his chance to become the prey! The hook found its destiny, and a stock standard Waterfall Way trout soon found its way into my net.

I took a quick photo, released the fish, then had a crazy idea – what if I could go for the trifecta today? The New England trout grand slam?

I worked out how long it would take me to get back to the car and to the brook trout spot, and from there I could do some more driving and stop in at my favourite rainbow trout creek before making the final leg of my journey home. I looked at my watch – time was now critical with the best half of the day already burnt. I clipped my caddis fly onto the hook catch on my rod and jogged back to the car through the misty rain. I opened the passenger door and placed my rod between the passenger seat and the centre console of the ute before racing around and jumping in and taking off towards the spot.

I stopped for diesel, a sausage roll, and an iced coffee from the servo, then jumped back in and kept moving. The sun was getting lower and the flaky pastry went everywhere as I devoured the sausage roll. But I soon turned down the unfamiliar road and came up to the creek crossing that Youngy had described. It was then I noticed that I wasn't the first person here – a Toyota Land

Cruiser ute with a couple of large breed pigging dogs on the steel tray were parked just off the road under the shade of a gum tree.

Downstream, three guys with fishing rods stood around a large hole in the creek. The afternoon sun was casting radiant golden light from behind them and I watched as one of them made a cast with what must have been a very cheap spinning rod, as big coils of monofilament line floated through the air like a giant clear slinky. My crushed spirit slowly lifted, as trout didn't often fall victim to such careless gear and technique. They were also a good 150m downstream, and I hadn't come this far to give up now – I'd just have to fish the small skinny water they had walked past.

The water was a milky nutrient-rich grey blue colour, so I decided to tie on a dropper nymph below my caddis.

Youngy had told me that the first fish they caught came right from under the outflow of a culvert under the bridge, so I went there first, considering that these three guys most likely walked straight past the bathtub-sized body of water.

After I cast, the fly rig landed right at the head of the pool, then halfway back towards me the caddis was sucked down by a fish that had grabbed the nymph below. The hook was set and the fight below the murky surface was on. This fish felt pretty solid and my heart was beginning to race at the thought of my first brook trout after all these years!

I was also trying to play the fish stealthily, so as to not draw attention from the three guys downstream. I even crouched down as if to look under the road, sneakily placed the landing net in front of me and gently coaxed the fish into it.

In slow motion, I lifted the still-submerged fish out of the water to get my first glimpse of the brook trout. I imagined the deep crimson red of its fins, accentuated by the clean white outlines, contrasting against the greens and purples of the body.

But once the fish came out of the water and stilled from its thrashing, there were no red fins.

Perhaps this was just a pale one, I tried to tell myself, but part of me knew this was just a run of the mill rainbow trout. I kept the fish in the net, took a quick photo, pulled the hook out and slid it back into the water. It was at this moment I knew one thing for almost certain: if I could find a brook trout now with the remaining afternoon light, I would complete the trifecta without having to detour via my go-to rainbow creek on the way home.

I stood up and turned around to see the three guys from downstream making their way towards their cruiser. They just gave a bit of a nod, kept walking and climbed in before kicking the V8 engine over. Then plumes of black smoke spilled out as they thundered up the road.

I fished where they had been, as it appeared to be the largest hole in the creek system, but even my best drifts went ignored. Downstream, the creek got narrower and narrower as it began to weave in tighter and tighter on itself like a python coiled around its kill. The creek even disappeared in sections under thick overhangs of tussock grass, which ruled out any conventional fly casting techniques, so bow and arrow casts and teabagging became the only viable option.

But the next hour rolled by and not even a darting glimpse of a fish, causing me to doubt my decision, even if I was in the right spot.

On the way back to the car in the fading light, I found a slightly wider, more open pool along the serpentine creek. I landed the fly and dropper at the head of the pool and moved the rod with my hand, slowly dragging it downstream to simulate a drift without the fly line itself in the water by dapping the fly.

One, two, three dabs and, as I went to lift the caddis off the surface again, it was dragged back under the surface before the coming storm of chaos caused by a deceived trout stung by a sharp hook played out.

I dipped the net under, coaxed the fish in, and it was all over in a very short amount of time.

This time I was certain. There was the deep crimson red of its fins, accentuated by the clean white outlines, contrasting against the greens and purples of the body. It was the brook trout I had dreamed of catching for years, and to my knowledge it was also the first time someone had completed the trout trifecta in New England. Maybe there have been others who have done it before I did, but they definitely kept it on the quiet.

After seeing and experiencing the creek and the small wild population, I don't blame them.

Chapter 17 – Life is Fine Between the Pines

The pine plantations around Hanging Rock have been a part of my outdoors playground since childhood. First with camping trips to Ponderosa Park with family and friends, and later on I started to hunt them under the R-license scheme (Restricted Game Hunting Licence), which allows recreational hunting on declared public land. I had fallen in love with the sweet smell of pines and how quiet they were to walk through on the hunt.

On one particular camping trip when my brother Mark and I were younger, we had taken some rods and bait to try and catch trout that were rumoured to be in the two dams at Ponderosa Park. It was late afternoon and we were drowning some earthworms in the bottom dam when I felt an unmistakable bite on my line.

I was soon in the midst of a great fight with what would have to have been a good trout! So you could rightly imagine the bewilderment and disappointment plainly painted on my face when I pulled an eel up the bank. We let it go peacefully and decided that the rumours of trout were of little value.

Years later, I heard other rumours of trout in the forest, but this time in some small and not so obvious creeks. I had just turned 16 when myself and my friend Tim had been given a tip-off about one such location, so we got dropped off one morning and organised a pickup for mid-afternoon the same day.

With nothing but a backpack with some water bottles, muesli bars and youthful ambition, we forged our way down the road and through the pines, only to discover a dry gully. We replayed the directions we had been given over and over again, trying to work out if we had misheard or been sent on a wild goose chase. First we backtracked down the sticky red forestry road, then we followed our noses downhill towards the smell of fresh water. We eventually found a small barely flowing stream about three inches deep and a foot wide, which was severely overgrown with brush and fallen debris from dead gums.

It was futile to even attempt fishing it, and when we backed out of the long grass, we each had a small legion of leeches attached to our boots and legs.

Taking refuge on the nearby gravel road, we began to remove the leeches, and eat all of our snacks within the first few hours.

With nothing else to do, we then put our fly rods together and began some casting practice on the deserted road. We compared the two rods and discussed what we didn't like about each – well, mostly what we didn't like about my heavy fiberglass composite rod. The casting practice improved our limited skills and helped to ward off boredom until our designated pick-up time.

CHAPTER 17 – LIFE IS FINE BETWEEN THE PINES

Two years later, however, after I had my P-plates and with a day off work on my calendar, I borrowed Mum's black Holden Jackaroo 4x4 for the day to explore, and set off with a rod just in case.

I drove that all familiar drive up into the forest, switched the Jackaroo into low range, and began descending down a rough rutted out forestry track. As I drove over rocks and smashed through puddles of red muddy water, I wondered whether I would have enough traction to get to the other side with the standard highway tyres fitted to the vehicle, but it surprisingly did with ease.

After I rounded a final corner on the descent, the pine trees opened up and revealed a gully lined with a mix of gums and pines. Winding the window down on the car, I could hear the unmistakable sound of running water over rocks, so wanted to pull over straight away but couldn't find anywhere to safely do so.

A little ways further down, however, I found a section of track just wide enough to safely park off the side. The sound of crashing water was more intense down here and the air was alive with bird calls in the mild autumn sun.

I decided to take just my small spinning rod with a spinner to see if I could attract any interest, if indeed there were any fish in the stream. The water was hardly visible from the track, sheathed by a veil of blackberries and fallen trees.

After some careful navigating, I found a large hole and managed a cast up under an overhanging branch. As I lifted the spinner out of the water, I heard a small splash and saw an unmistakable silver flash out of my peripheral vision. I repeated the cast, had the same result and realised that the fish was barely fingerling size.

So, moving on from that pool, I found a section of creek easier to walk along, as the blackberries couldn't grow on the solid rock banks. I had similar results in each hole, but couldn't find anything big enough to fit the treble in its mouth.

When upstream became too tough to bush bash through, I turned back around and went to the car, to see if I could find another access point. This involved me crossing the creek and creeping slowly along in the car, until the road ahead began to turn into ultra deep red mud ruts full of water. I got out to inspect them on foot, probing the bottom with a stick, and knew I wouldn't be able to get through this obstacle. But now the only option was to attempt a 100-point turn on the narrow track or reverse all the way back out.

I attempted the 100-point turn and, on the second forward turn, the front wheels went over the edge of the track into some soft ground. I quickly put it into reverse and, to my horror, the front end began to bury down – the vehicle didn't move backwards at all!

Assessing the situation from the outside revealed I was in a bad spot if I couldn't somehow free myself. I was getting ready to call for help when I happened to glance at the instructions for

CHAPTER 17 – LIFE IS FINE BETWEEN THE PINES

switching into 4x4 mode on a sticker in the car. That was when I realised this whole time I had only been running in two-wheel drive, as I hadn't engaged the 4x4 system properly!

Once I heard the 4x4 system engage, I put the car back into reverse – it crawled straight out and I was free. After that I called it a day, though resolved to come back in a year or two when the fingerling sized fish would hopefully be bigger.

Sitting down with my older brother Mark after our trip away with Youngy and Erro, I told him about the creek and my keenness to get back and check on the growth of the tiny trout. A plan was made and we set off in my silver Mazda Bravo, arriving not long after sunrise.

Climbing up the mountain is always a special experience, as the air gets colder and the smell of pine wafts through the rattling dust-lined vents of the ute. It was the same on this trip and, as we turned a corner, rays of sun caressed the dew laden tops of the pines in a chromatic aura, while simultaneously casting a dark shadow over the steep deep gully below, into which we were about to drive.

We rattled and rolled down the steep tracks before finding a section of track just wide enough to pull over and park, without rolling down the side of the hill. Here in the gully, the sun wasn't yet breaking through, so we got our gear together in a pre-dawn shadow, while the wind gently whispered through the pines.

The brisk air was strong but not unpleasant against my face – perfect autumn conditions. A few hundred metres from the ute, I spotted a deciduous tree of some kind, turned full golden and threatening to shed its leaves, surrounded by an unmoving honour guard of evergreen pines. In the same moment that I spotted it, sun rays began to break through the pines and the small tree began to blaze. It was breath-taking.

Since we parked, we had been able to hear the creek, but hadn't been able to see it through the undergrowth of blackberry and ferns. But as the sun broke through, we could see the green gold shimmer of its surface on the gully floor, twisting in and around large rocks as it meandered down the gully.

In this we became the water, as we meandered along the narrow path, shadowing the creek in and out of blackberry bushes in the hopes of our paths joining.

Our hopes came to fulfillment as we took a step down towards the creek edge, and onto some rocks sitting in the stream.

I had been tying some small gold bead nymphs and was keen to test them out some more, so I tied on a size sixteen and, with my four-weight, I made a cast to the head of the pool, mending the line through my left hand I felt a tension and lifted into it, only to have a small fingerling sized trout get launched from the water and land at my feet.

CHAPTER 17 – LIFE IS FINE BETWEEN THE PINES

We criss-crossed the stream to the next bend, trying our best to get away from the blackberries and find relatively fishable water, which was proving to be very difficult. Mark managed to find a slightly better sized trout from a section of shallow water going over bowling ball sized rocks scattered throughout the hole. But there was only one rock to stand on, amongst a clearing in the blackberries, so once Mark had landed his and released it back to the grey murky water, we swapped places on the rock pedestal.

I worked the pool thoroughly and was about to move on when the line came up tight, right as the leader was at the tip of my rod. A very energetic rainbow cut zig zags amongst the rocks before finally expending all her energy and slipping into the net!

From here on, there was less and less accessible water due to fallen trees, blackberries and steep clay Swiss cheese banks, indicating a large population of resident crayfish. Flipping some rocks in a shallow section of creek, I found a finger-length crayfish, red in colour and its body covered in small spines. Very different from the typical smooth black and blue crays we were used to finding.

By this point, the sun was very high in the sky and, after leap-frogging across a shallow section of water, we made our way back to the ute. We rattled and rolled our way back up the mountain and decided to take a back dirt road home.

Halfway down the mountain, however, I caught the movement of something on my knee while I was driving. A dirty big leech was trying to traverse my leg and find an opening to take his fill!

Not wanting to stop on the sketchy narrow gravel road, I asked Mark to grab my multi tool pliers, grab it, and chuck it out the window.

I've always been a fan of taking home souvenirs from adventures, I'd just prefer to pick them myself!

Chapter 18 – Sheba Shenanigans

September 2013

A large part of my childhood was spent fishing the dams within an hour or two of where I grew up. There was Chaffey, which provided part of Tamworth's water supply, and which was full of carp, Murray cod, Golden Perch and Silver Perch. Holding the same species was Lake Keepit, which was mostly used as water storage for farm irrigation.

But higher up in the mountains were two other dams – remnants from Nundle's gold rush years. The dams are surrounded by native forest with a scattering of pine trees, which reveal their more man-made origins, and are known as the 'Sheba Dams'.

I always preferred fishing there with Dad as a kid. I didn't know if it was the smell of the damp native forest, the little creek full of crayfish that connected the two dams, the more scenic setting, or the bigger-sized trout that called the dams home… It all makes sense now, even though the trout often tasted 'muddy'.

The second dam, or bottom dam as it is often referenced, is where I caught my first trout as a kid, sinking a worm we had hand dug that morning from our backyard compost in Werris Creek.

A few years later, I caught my first trout on a spinner, casting to the shallows near the outlet of the bottom dam.

We never really caught anything out of the top dam, but we also never fished it as much as the bottom dam. It had always been a bit of a boom and bust fishery to us – some days you wouldn't even get a bite and others you would land a half-dozen healthy rainbows between myself, Dad, and Mark.

Fast forward to being a young adult and talking with the right people, we soon found out that the stocking scheme for the dams had changed, with fisheries opting to stock the dams with large broodstock trout from the hatchery at Ebor, as opposed to the traditional stocking of fingerlings.

The stocking of the dams was typically done at the end of the breeding season, August to October, with an even amount in each dam. Once word got out that the stocking truck had been, there was a silent race from locals to catch some as quickly as possible. We usually opted to avoid the circus and focus our efforts on the smarter fish that survived the first wave.

It was around this time that I had befriended a group of doctors and physios doing their residencies and placements at the Tamworth hospital. A couple of them had gone in the first wave to have a crack and managed to get some nice fish on the fly rod stripping wet flies from the banks of the top dam. I had caught plenty of fish there but never on fly. So I went to the local tackle store and loaded up on some Mrs Simpson, Matukas, and Tungsten woolly buggers before heading up the mountain with some guys from work, and Dave or 'Straighty' – as the physio with impeccable posture was affectionately known.

The advice from the other guys was simple: find a spot and just strip away until a trout passes by on his 'beat'. So I picked a fallen tree on the opposite side of the dam, and stood on the red clay among the tree's exposed roots, which gave me a clear view of the tree's limbs and branches amongst the discoloured water.

About five minutes later, I saw a pasty white silhouette go under the trunk below me and realised it was a nice-sized trout making his beat. I quickly retrieved the Mrs Simpson and redirected a cast to intercept him, but he caught my movement and was gone in a flash.

The next few hours passed in a delirium of rhythmic casting myself into a catatonic state. The sun was almost at noon now, we had all had an encounter with a trout but had all failed to land one. Then I landed a cast beyond the end of the sunken tree's tallest branches, the little dark fly making a 'plop' sound and beginning to descend into the murk, although illuminated by a little ray of sunshine amongst the shadows of the giant gum trees.

Having pushed myself into a meditative state, I began to visualise what it would be like to see a big hook jaw buck rainbow emerge from the depths, smash the fly and retreat back to his hidey hole at the end of the fallen tree.

That was when my mental and physical worlds collided and, exactly as I had seen in my mind, a big buck rainbow emerged from the depths, inhaled the fly, and with a quick flick from his tail, depth-charged back to his home at the end of the tree.

I was in shock and awe, letting out a cry of excitement followed by a crushing cry of defeat when the line flicked back towards me slack. The trout had stolen my dreams and my new fly.

I probably would have fished until it got dark, and possibly after, but the others were keen to get home. I vowed to come back as soon as I could.

I didn't have to wait long. By midweek I had organised to go up again with one of the young doctors who was keen to get one, after his mates had all caught some and he was feeling left out. Ben, or 'Wags' as we called him, had first reached out to me when he moved to Tamworth and was looking for some flies and advice. Having moved down from the Northern Territory, he was a keen Barramundi angler but was looking to get in amongst some trout on the fly.

At this time of my life, I was now doing a metal fabrication apprenticeship, which meant 6am starts and 2:45pm finishes. So I packed all my gear into the ute the night before and, as soon as I clocked out for the afternoon, I picked Ben up and we made the hour-long drive from Tamworth to the dams.

It was late afternoon when we arrived, just an hour or two of light left at the most, as the sun was already beginning to dip behind the gums. We climbed into our waders and made our way to a spot not too far from where I had been the previous Saturday. The dam was at least empty of people – no one was camped and no one was enjoying a picnic up on the shore. This in itself filled me with hope that we had a good chance of finding some fish in our small window of light.

Either way, we had arrived in time for golden hour and the surface of the dam was flat and embossed in a golden chrome from the late afternoon sun.

Making our way to the far shore, we picked a spot about ten metres apart, a safe distance to cast but still able to have a chat as we got into our repetitive casting, just hoping a trout came into our firing lines.

We weren't there long when Wags said he had a hit, but then his line went slack and our hopes faded, albeit momentarily as we then saw the slab of a hen rainbow breach the water in three successive leaps, rivalling that of a dolphin. We watched on gobsmacked until I noticed Wags' line peeling sharply to the right, following the leaping trout.

"I think you are hooked up to that!" I exclaimed.

Hooked up he was, and the trout fought to the very end.

I didn't typically wear waders when I fished this dam due to the steep banks in places, but I was glad to be wearing them that day as it allowed me to net the fish for Wags with ease. I snapped some photos in the water and we began to revive the fish and release. She was very spent after the fight but eventually came too and swam off. I felt a mixture of guilt – if she died there to become yabby food – but also filled with hope that she would live and make some young angler's day.

After all the commotion of catching that fish, I came to terms with the fact that I might not get a fish myself, but enjoyed being out there regardless.

The sun had just set when I was mid strip of the fly line, when it came up tight and peeled out the opposite way. Blind casting often leaves you in a delirious fog, but when the fish do hit, you become reanimated, like slowly regaining consciousness, becoming suddenly aware of your surroundings and what you were doing. It was the same for me as the fish had me snapping quickly back into focus. It did none of the acrobatics of Wags' fish, and gave up its fight very quickly. He was also the ugliest trout I'd ever caught – a big hook jaw ground at the bottom from spending most of his life on the bottom of a concrete hatchery tank. His tail was only half there and he had a little fin on one side, just like Nemo from the Disney movie.

A quick donk on the head put him out of his misery and we called it an afternoon. Both of us were keen to have a counter meal and cold beer at the Nundle pub, a beautiful classic Australian pub right on the corner of the two main streets.

We arrived at the pub right at last light. Locals in hi-vis were washing away the work day around the solid tables out the front, others were playing a game of pool inside. When we went to order our meals, we were prompted to do so sooner rather than later as the kitchen would be closing soon. That seemed to be a running theme on my fishing trips, but when the fish are on, they are on, and I'd willingly miss out on dinner than make it to a pub before the kitchen cut off, fully aware of the consequences of my choices.

Looking back over photos of the fish we had just caught, Wags decided to upload some to social media because this was his new personal best trout by a long shot.

After we ate, we left for Tamworth, and then I remembered I had to work in the morning. The trout I was going to give the foreman would hopefully grant me enough brownie points next time I wanted to leave early for a fish!

Right before bed, my phone dinged with a notification. One of Wags' mates, Richard, had tagged him and myself in a photo. He had removed the slab of a rainbow trout from Wags' hands in the photo and replaced it with an elongated self-portrait.

I thought, "Who needs enemies when you have friends like this?", then went to bed.

A few weeks later, Sarah, who was now my fiancé, came with me to go up to the dams for a picnic. Just out of Nundle, I saw a sign for Antimony Mine and a small area of road shoulder in which we could park. I'd always wanted to check this out, so we parked the ute and went for a closer inspection.

The mine entrance was now a small opening that you had to hunch over to enter, which then opened into another section with a daylight shaft cut up before going into a long strip mine that you could comfortably stand in, as long as you weren't claustrophobic or scared of the dark. We didn't have a proper torch, but each had a small light on our phones. Still, the darkness was so overwhelming you couldn't see more than a few paces in front.

Having satisfied my curiosity, we got back in the ute and made our way up the short steep winding road to Hanging Rock.

We arrived to find the place empty, which was unusual for a weekend. Instead of fishing the steep banks we took advantage of the jetty free of people. I let Sarah fish right off the end and into the better water, while I focused my efforts on the shallower water, part-way out along the jetty. I was fishing my six-weight, which is a lovely handmade rod from Peter and Tony of HCE Fly Rods in Melbourne. It made casting the weighted woolly bugger I had tied on much more enjoyable.

On my first cast I felt tension for a split second and thought maybe the fly had fouled in the shallow water. I was even starting to think that perhaps the weighted fly was the wrong choice for the shallower water alongside the jetty. But after casting into the same spot over and over and over again, I never felt the same thing.

Having this realisation, I told Sarah I was sure that I had had a missed strike. She usually out fished me and hadn't even had a bite, so she was sceptical to say the least. But sure enough, a few casts later I felt the tension through the fly line as it lightly stripped back through my fingers. I pulled against it briefly before lifting the rod and the tension of the line shook loose droplets of water, showering the glassy water below.

I couldn't tell if it was a good-sized fish at first or not, but every time I thought it was getting close, it went for a run back out into the deeper water. Realising I wasn't going to be able to lift it out of the water onto the jetty, I made a quick dash down the hardwood planks and onto the small sandy 'beach' beside it. I only had a small handled landing net, and when I finally managed to get the fish's head into the net and lift it out of the water, barely half of the fish was within the net! The rest of its scaly writhing mass was in the open air above.

Overwhelmed and flabbergasted by what I was seeing, I began to laugh. You always look at pictures of big trout in magazines and online, but until you see a big hook jaw rainbow like this in the flesh it always seems like an impossibility.

Sarah had taken some videos of me landing it and decided she wanted to get some photos of us with the fish as well. Holding up her smartphone in selfie mode, I held the fish up between us as we huddled around the camera. She pressed the button on her screen and, as soon as she did, the fish decided the fight wasn't over until it's over, and slapped me across the face with its head, managing to put some of its slime in my mouth.

I spent the next few seconds spitting to try to remove it.

Not long after, Sarah laughed out loud. "You know how I tried to take a selfie just now? Well, I accidentally pressed the video button!" Then she held up her phone and a short clip of the fish headbutting me, followed by me spitting the taste out of my mouth, played on repeat.

Some moments you never forget, and some moments – even if you do forget them – social media memories will have you reliving them each year when the day passes.

This is one of those memories and I always look back on it fondly.

Chapter 19 – Fireflies

December 2013

Not long after the cool August and September months had passed with some memorable sessions at Sheba Dams, the days were growing longer and hotter and I was itching to head up to the Ebor area to escape the heat of Tamworth.

One Friday afternoon, I finished work at my metal fabrication job and, after washing off layers of grinding dust, I set off for the shops. First stop was the tackle store. I needed some leader material and some more lures for Sarah. Then, passing a picnic bag with an inbuilt cooler, I had an idea…

Sarah and I were engaged and a date was set for the wedding the following year, but, aware of just how lucky I was to be marrying her, I wanted to keep her impressed. So I picked out some wine at the bottle shop, some cheese and crackers from the deli, and took it all home for the next day.

I spent that evening getting rods rigged and had a chat with Wags about a spot I had mentioned to him, but had never fished with fly gear before, whereas he had recently gotten into fly tying and with hands fit for a surgeon he had tied up some small Parachute Adams flies, which he graciously gave me a few. It felt a bit surreal to be given some flies from someone who had bought flies off me less than a year ago, just starting out on his fly fishing journey. His flies were nicely proportioned and were definitely catching fish.

If there is one thing I've learnt about getting people into fishing and wanting them to enjoy it, is that you need to have everything ready to go so all they have to do is cast and enjoy the scenery. So I had the ute packed the night before once the rods were rigged, and following a well-earned sleep in on the Saturday morning, I went and picked up Sarah and we started making our way up the New England Highway.

Glorious was the only way to describe the conditions. It was warm and an early afternoon sun was beaming all around. Turning onto a gravel road and driving into the towering eucalypts, the cicadas began to sing in a deafening rendition of the Australian summer anthem. A large pale dust cloud followed us down the road, indicating it hadn't rained in the past few days so the water should be clear and we might have a chance of sight-fishing for a change.

Turning off the gravel road, we were greeted by tall tree ferns peppered throughout the undergrowth of the pale barked snow gums. I got out of the ute to engage the hubs before putting the vehicle into low range and slowly descending down to the valley floor.

The spot we were heading for could be a bit hit and miss. Sometimes it was a popular camp spot and – as I would later find out after recommending it to a mate in the area – sometimes it was a popular spot for a bush doof! That particular mate, Luke, had driven down one afternoon and found droves of the great unwashed doing psychedelics and grooving to music down by the river as they made rock cairns.

Thankfully, however, as I shut the ute door behind me, I was greeted with the chaotic silence of the Australian bush, cicadas and birds in full song, a gentle breeze through the tree canopy high overhead, and the sound of running water over freestones in the river, now just mere metres away.

I decided it was best to park as far upstream as I could, then walk downstream as far as we were willing to fish, and work our way back to the ute. Luckily a fire trail shadowed the river for a while, which made this an easy option.

Coming around a corner on the fire trail, we got our first glimpse of the river for the day and I almost couldn't believe my eyes. Right there in the shade of a tree was a bunch of trout! We took another step and they all scattered. Upstream and downstream, everywhere in between, and some who probably hadn't seen what the disturbance was, did a few more laps of the pool in confusion.

I had never seen the water here so clear! The moon and stars must have truly aligned on this day. Truth be told, we didn't walk too far. There is a saying that 'you don't leave fish to find fish', so we only made our way 200 or so metres past the pool where we had spoked the fish. Mostly to give them a chance to settle down and hopefully be hungry by the time we came back through.

After taking a shortcut through some tall grass that parted like a curtain revealing the river below, we hit the edge of the bank. Down here the trees surrounding the river were a little thicker and arched their way over like a gauntlet designed to intimidate the budding fly fisher. Moss lined rocks on the opposite bank, and the occasional bonk of a frog could be heard escaping from their hiding spots by the water. The side closest to us had bigger freestones, which were bleached from the overhead sun, and when we took a closer look we could see people had been stacking them into impressive little cairns of seemingly impossible balance, which seemed to defy gravity and the laws of nature.

I had chosen not to wear waders and that proved to be the right decision as I stepped into the water and felt the cool relief of the crystal clear water against my feet and calves. I ushered Sarah ahead of me to give her the best chance of catching the first fish. Standing midstream, she landed a nice cast at the base of a larger boulder that was terracing the water between this pool and the next. A few short turns of the reel and the magic – which you always hope to happen but seldom does – began to unfurl before our eyes with a small trout getting airborne.

With all its fins perfectly intact, I suspected this rainbow was of wild stock, or at least a fry or fingerling release that had grown up in the wild.

CHAPTER 19 – FIREFLIES

As quick as it was to hand and admired, it was released back into the clear cold water.

Around the next bend, there was a large pool of water about the length of a tennis court and a few metres deep against the far bank, with large overhanging trees to give shade and root structure. We thought there must certainly be a thumper of a trout lurking in there somewhere, but not through lack of trying we were unable to entice him out from wherever he may have been hiding.

I toyed with the idea of one day returning with a snorkel and diving the deeper bank with a torch to have a thorough look, but maybe that would ruin some of the magic of imagining the big trout that may or may not exist, and perhaps in cases like this it is better for the sake of mystery to be a man of faith and not of science.

The sun was starting to descend by now but it was still filling the summer air with its warmth. We came to a section of river that was running mostly wide and shallow, except for a deeper shaded pocket at the head of the pool on the opposite undercut bank. The water between us and this shaded pocket was just over ankle deep and running clear, slow, and radiating the afternoon golden light.

From this distance it was too hard for me to land a cast into the zone, so in true gentleman fashion I offered it to Sarah.

She made probably one of the best casts I've seen, her little lure making a subtle 'plop' in the rippling white water. I watched the end of her green braided line and when I saw the leader come out of the shade and into the light, shortly followed by the lure, I could see a brown trout following it.

The fish followed it until she was within a few metres of us, then decided to turn around. I expected her to disappear back into the safety of her shady bank, but instead she swam a little downstream and just sat there, basking in the afternoon sun.

Sarah made a few more casts but she had gone lockjaw and wasn't budging. Sarah told me to make a cast instead and I didn't hesitate. I landed the bigger Royal Humpy and nymph rig a few feet in front.

The brown drew close to the fly, inspecting it with wild curiosity and terse disdain, then swam away. She never went far, though, and was just lazily cruising through the pool now. I dared not take my eyes off her in case I couldn't find her again in amongst the shadows and highlights of the river rocks below.

I quickly cut the humpy-nymph rig off and, looking in my box, saw one of Wags' small Parachute Adams in the top and remembered this was what he had used to land some nice fish. I threaded the line through the tiny eyelet, though it took several attempts with my semi-shaking hands before finally getting it through, wetting the line with my saliva, and pulling the knot tight.

A quick trim of the tail of the knot with the clippers, a small dab of floatant around the hackle, then honing back in on her I made the cast.

CHAPTER 19 – FIREFLIES

I cast further in front this time – a good six feet. The water wasn't running fast in this section of the river so I didn't have to worry about mending the line for the current.

The brown turned on the spot, sensing my offering balancing in the surface tension of the water. The tension between us grew, she was hopeful that what had landed in her domain was food and not a deception. Every fibre of my being prayed she would not see the lie. She slowly rose from the rocks and I could see every brown spot on her flank, her jaw threatening to break the tension, but perfectly preserving it as her mouth opened behind my fly. Her jaws closed in acceptance.

I broke the tension myself – lifting the rod. She was furious. She raged out across the golden surface of the water, crossing in and out of the two realms.

I had one last trick to deliver, and I slid the net down into the water while she faced away, before quickly leading her head back to the net. She was a beautiful little brown trout, cunning and discerning, and after I gently swam her away I have no doubt that she would question each meal more thoroughly than she had today.

It was now really late in the afternoon and, having meandered our way back upstream to the ute, we decided to push on a touch further upstream, if for no other reason than to see what was around the next bend.

We entered into a spectacular section of pocket water. Tall pale gums lined the banks, throwing their outstretched hands over the scattering of giant-sized marbles equally spaced throughout the river. Clear water wrapped around each of them before slinking away downstream, while the smells of damp earth and eucalyptus were strong in the air as the birds let out their final songs for the day.

A small clump of razor grass also hung out over the edge of the water, the underside of its roots providing a sneaky hidey hole in the bathtub-sized pocket of water. Its sandy gravel bottom was a luminous white gold, even though it was likely to be ankle deep.

I instructed Sarah to make a cast and she managed to land her small lure at the head of the pool, and right as it was near out of the water again a black shadow hastened out from the grass, grabbed the lure briefly before spitting it out nonchalantly and disappeared into his hidey hole. We tried again to get him to reappear, as he was a very solid fish, but our attempts were in vain.

It would be the last trout we saw for the day, but we were oblivious to that fact as only those truly living in the present can. We hopped our way upstream from rock to rock, making casts in each little pocket of water, criss-crossing across the large marble boulders. But then the sun disappeared behind the rim of the valley and the sky above the treetops was aflame in a melody of purple and orange, translucent over a clear blue sky.

The decision was made to start heading back before it got too dark. I mentioned we should be able to take a shortcut through the bush to the side and follow a small game trail back to the ute.

CHAPTER 19 – FIREFLIES

Sarah rolled her eyes at the suggestion of another one of my 'shortcuts'. The last time I had suggested something similar we had been covered head-to-toe in sticky beaks and ended up throwing away some clothes because not all of them could be removed. So I couldn't really blame her.

Pushing aside razor grass, lifting up low lying branches and just generally trying to clamber up the bank with brute force, we finally broke through into the game trail beyond the thick vegetation of the river's edge. Dodging small vines and trying not to trip over fallen logs was tiring work in the rapidly fading light.

After what seemed to be hours, but was most likely ten minutes, we entered a clearing and saw the silver ute there, its colour barely discernible in the low light. We brushed off the small sticks caught in our clothes and hair before packing away our rods, and pulling out the picnic bag and blanket. I poured some wine and we sat in the darkness, listening to the river on its eternal journey downstream, the frogs calling out in an out-of-time but melodic rhythm. An owl hooted in the distance. The air was clear and crisp. We chatted about the fish we had seen and caught, how beautiful the clear flowing water was, and more in general about life, work and the upcoming wedding. I took in a deep breath, smelling the fresh water, the damp earth and the eucalyptus forest hanging all around us. Looking at Sarah, I saw something flicker over her left shoulder in the blackness beyond, then another over the right. It took me a little while to process what was going on.

"Look behind you, Sarah! Fireflies!" I exclaimed. I had only ever seen them once before, when camping at Oxley Wild Rivers as a kid with my family.

"I've never seen them before!" Sarah said.

For the next hour we just sat, hand-in-hand gazing upon the firefly galaxy that had appeared under the thick of the canopy of old growth gums around us, stars visible beyond, intertwining with the flicker and flashes of these fascinating insects creating their own cosmos.

Chapter 20 – New Parents

On the 30th of August 2014, I woke early after a restless sleep. I still wasn't used to our new house. It was the first house I had ever rented, since neither Sarah nor I had lived away from our parental homes and I had been paying board to stay in a spare room at Sarah's parents place up until a few days prior to getting the keys to this house.

I stepped out into the kitchen, which was mostly empty space as we had no furniture yet, and that was just as well because it meant there was room for some of my mates to sleep in various parts of the house in sleeping bags and air mattresses on the floor. I crept over to the fridge and picked out some bacon, and a tray of eggs. Grabbing the fresh buns from the bench and some BBQ sauce, I then made my way to the glass sliding door at the back of the house and onto the concrete alfresco area outside where there was a BBQ. I left the glass door open and shut the sliding screen door to allow the smell to waft through the house. I figured this was easier than ripping blankets off people and telling them to wake up. Like zombies rising from the grave, they all eventually stirred once the bacon had finished cooking and the buns lightly toasted.

We had only just finished eating when someone knocked on the door.

I opened it to find the wedding photographers there to get some photos of us all getting ready. The big day had finally arrived!

It was a glorious blue sky day, typical of the end of winter in the North West of New South Wales. The temperature was mild and the first of spring's blossoms were popping in a dazzling and fragrant display of pink and white, which coincidentally matched the colour scheme we had chosen for the wedding.

Although I'm not a big believer in coincidence, I don't think for a second that Sarah and I met coincidentally, or that we coincidentally picked colours that complemented the season perfectly, or that we had timed our wedding to the day of the arrival of the Heritage Express steam train to Tamworth. No, this couldn't all be coincidence. We were dealing with fate.

Myself, Jason, Mark, Beau, Matt, and Sarah's brothers Josh and Michael waited in the front pew of Saint Patrick's Catholic Church, West Tamworth. A mid-afternoon sun was beaming through the stained glass window beside us, casting a radiant glow over myself and the groomsmen. I took it as a sign that currently I was right where God had intended me to be, and when I turned and saw Sarah walking down the aisle with her father, it wasn't just a sign – it was confirmation.

CHAPTER 20 – NEW PARENTS

A few days later we packed the car with some suitcases and fishing rods, and began our journey to North Stradbroke Island. Neither of us had been before, so didn't quite know what to expect. We passed over trout streams that we couldn't fish as the season was closed, but we were already dreaming about getting back to our local haunts in a little over a month's time.

After driving off the vehicular ferry from Cleveland, we touched down onto the sealed roads of the island, and began the short drive to Point Lookout on its other side. Even the name of the town made me think about trout fishing, given it shared the name of the lookout at Ebor, close to some great fishing in the Styx River.

We picked up the keys to our holiday rental, then drove up the hill to the house. I soon realised that the pictures online had way undersold this place! There were 180 degree views of the Pacific Ocean, which was mesmerising from up high. We could watch as the swell gently rolled through over the great expanse and crashed against a bommie not far from the shore.

We all but threw our suitcases inside before heading straight back out and down to the nearest beach. Eight-weight fly rod in hand with a small Clouser ready, I wasn't sure what to expect.

Soon, a dark cloud appeared beneath the water and rolled towards where we were standing on the beach. From afar, black torpedoes then launched towards it, cruising in at pace within the waves. The cloud now pinned between the shore had nowhere to go. The cloud turned into a churning of silver and black as bait fish panicked to escape the dolphins who had bested them yet again.

A few swipes through from each of them and it was all over. The dolphins rolled back out to deeper water, allowing me to cast to where the bait ball had been not expecting much. I began stripping the line back through my fingers, until the line pulled taut. I set the hook and the fish began to cut rapidly along the wave. The midday sun occasionally reflected off of its silver flanks. I timed a wave crashing up the beach to extract the fish from the ocean, and had it beached.

A decent-sized swallow tail dart lay in the sand flicking its big forked tail. They look sort of like a miniature permit, probably why they got the nickname 'poor man's permit'.

I caught a few more and slipped them into our small orange esky.

Then I hung the fly on the rod, wound in the slack line, cleaned the fish and we made our way back along the beach to the car.

We had to walk past three men fishing along the same gutter, all of whom had been fishing everything from fresh beach worms, pipis and strip baits without so much as a nibble in the entire hour we had spent there. It's not every day you can out-fish the bait guys on fly gear but you have to take the wins when you can get them.

Back at the holiday house, I prepared the fish by making a few diagonal slices into the fillets on each side and, after giving them a light dusting of flour, salt, and pepper, shallow fried them in some olive oil. Plated up with some fresh salad, they were deliciously fresh, with crispy skin and subtle flavour.

People sometimes avoid this fish for the table because they are too 'fiddly' to fillet, but cooked whole once gutted, and being willing to pick the meat off the frame will definitely yield rewards.

We sat out on the upstairs alfresco. The ocean was a deep blue as the sun dipped behind the horizon – a deep blue of gently rolling swell, the southernmost point of Moreton Island just visible. The air was pleasant and clean with a gentle sea breeze coming off the ocean and up the hill to the house. It was quite a sight and the house we were staying in was far too big for the two of us, but we had rented it for the view and certainly got our money's worth.

We talked about the day over the fresh dart, enjoying each other's company. We discussed how amazing this island was and how relatively cheap it was to come here compared to other places. It certainly was a hidden gem. Discussing the fishing, we decided it had been good, and the scenery here was stunning... But deep down we were both dreaming of being back in a clear freshwater stream surrounded by rainforest and fiery trout.

We left Straddie and headed inland to the university in Toowoomba where Sarah would be doing a practical for her nursing studies. I killed some time by walking around the university campus, inspired by its size. I felt a boost of inspiration to maybe one day do a degree myself, but I had no idea what, if anything I would study.

A few months later, I came home from a day at my apprenticeship – which I was set to finish at the end of the year – and felt very unfulfilled. Sarah and I were eating dinner when the phone rang. It was Sarah's brother Michael. Sarah kept looking at me as she chatted away on the phone and I returned her some puzzled looks as I heard my name mentioned.

Turns out, the local surveying and engineering firm he was working for were looking for a new survey assistant and draftsman. I had a few questions, mostly regarding pay and educational opportunities as I was keen to learn something new, but went for a job interview later that week and got the position! Within six months I was enrolled into a Bachelor of Spatial Science (Surveying) through the same university where I had been just a few months prior.

In August the following year, just weeks before our first wedding anniversary, we welcomed James into our family. We had talked about going back to 'Straddie' but, not long after we had been, Point Lookout Beach was voted one of the best beaches in Australia. The hidden gem was rinsed of its mud and revealed for the diamond it truly was, making it no longer an option for our small family while I worked and studied surveying via distance education.

CHAPTER 20 – NEW PARENTS

The day after James was born, I found myself very sleep deprived sitting in the soft lighting of the maternity ward, after a very long couple of days that had ended in an emergency caesarean. Sarah and James were fast asleep and I pulled out my laptop to finish and proofread my first university assignment. I uploaded and submitted it before finally leaning back and getting a few winks of sleep. This was the beginning of a very stressful and tiring seven-year period of my life. Like most things worth doing, you cannot obtain the reward without a certain degree of difficulty and suffering.

A few months later, after a big week of work, I was eating breakfast and sipping my black coffee when my right eye began to twitch. I knew this was a sign my body and mind needed a reset and, when Sarah emerged from our room a short time later, I proposed that we pack the car and drive to Ebor.

We were both tired beyond measure adjusting to being new parents for the first time, but we needed to get out and about to break up some of the monotony. The first hour and a half of travel went smoothly and we made it to Armidale with James barely making a sound from his baby seat in the back of our small SUV.

We got some coffee before continuing out along the Waterfall Way. Fifteen minutes later, James cracked it and started screaming. Just down the road we found a rest area and pulled over to sort him out. A quick nappy change, something to eat, and a cuddle from Sarah and he was back to normal. But he wanted to crawl around inside the car before getting back in his seat. This was going to be a long day!

I'd given a lot of thought on the drive up about accessibility to the various streams around Ebor, and had decided to fish one of the highest fished places in the area. We turned off to the left just before Ebor and made our way to the Upper Falls carpark.

The fields either side of the entrance to the national park were a melody of green and white with everlasting daisies in amongst the gums. There wasn't anyone else in sight, which was a good sign, so I unloaded James' pram from the boot, grabbed the picnic bag and rods, and we strolled our way upstream along the walking track.

A few hundred metres up, we found an opening in the trees and a section where the path was close to the river. I pushed down on the back of the pram to lift the front wheels, as I turned it off the asphalt path and onto the grass.

There was a nice spot clear of long grass with some mossy rocks and shorter grass that looked ideal to set up the picnic. I pulled the picnic blanket out from the bottom of the pram and spread it out.

James was keen to get out of the pram and, as soon as I placed him onto the mat, he began to turn and crawl off the edge, determined to be anywhere but on the confines of the mat.

When Sarah took a seat, James at least crawled over to her while I took the food out of our picnic basket. We had an assortment of leftover BBQ chicken wings, drumsticks, and fresh pasta salad.

CHAPTER 20 – NEW PARENTS

We scoffed down what we could whilst also steering James away from the water and back onto the picnic blanket. Then I packed the containers away and swapped them for my fly rod.

James was only happy with me holding him, so I carried him in my left arm, fly rod in the right, and carefully made my way down to the edge of the river. I set myself up an easy casting distance below the head of a run, and began to cast my dry fly and nymph combo to the top of the run.

The first cast was less than ideal and the flies landed in a haphazard mess about half way up.

James let out a small cry as he slowly sagged down my hip. I pulled him back up high on my hip and made another cast. This cast was better, the flies landing right where I had imagined. They began to drift as expected, until the dry went under. I lifted the rod expecting a fish and found only weed.

I cast again and had the same problem. With James in one arm and the rod tucked under my other arm, I managed to bite the nymph off and shorten the tippet connecting the nymph to dry by about 100mm and tie it back on. Still cradling James on my left hip, I awkwardly pulled some fly line out and made the cast again.

They landed true and began drifting.

I watched with anticipation, imagining a fish grabbing either fly at any moment.

The dry went under.

I lifted, and this time the receiving end of the line came alive! A small rainbow trout going hard, furious at her mistake.

The line went slack.

She was gone.

A quick roll cast to the same spot.

I watched the flies drift.

James began to slide down my hip again. I pulled him back up, but when I looked back up I couldn't see the dry.

I lifted. A new trout was on the end, maybe slightly bigger though it was hard to tell.

"Net please!" I called out to Sarah.

A few missed net attempts later and we managed to get her into the net. A very small rainbow, probably a few centimetres undersized.

I didn't even notice at the time, but somewhere in the chaos my eye had stopped twitching. I worked the same little stretch of water for another twenty minutes or so, and still managed to find a few trout, one was even willing enough to eat the dry.

James started to get unbearably restless, though, and we knew our time was up.

Sarah also had a go fishing while I had James on my hip but hadn't managed to hook anything on spin gear. The fish in this section definitely saw their fair share of lures over the course of a season.

I felt bad that she hadn't caught anything, but we would certainly try again when the season reopened.

Chapter 21 – Three Weekends, Three Species

Trout Opening 2016

It was a gloomy September Saturday afternoon and it had been raining for what felt like forever. James was fast asleep in his cot, Sarah was at work at the nursing home, and I was at my tying desk spinning thread, dubbing, hair, and feathers. The NSW season opened the following weekend and I was making the most of my down time by preparing my gear and restocking depleted flies, mostly Elk Hair Caddis, Parachute Adams, and bead head nymphs.

I snipped a pinch of elk hair, daydreamed about one bugling deep in a backcountry gully in Montana with a bow in my hand, placed it in the stacker and pulled out a neat bunch of perfectly aligned hairs. Pinching them above the almost complete fly in the vise with my left hand, I wrapped them down with some thread with the bobbin in my right hand. I was firm enough to pull the hairs down and secure them, but not so firm as to snap the thread. The hair fibres began to kick up and take on the shape of a caddis wing. After a few whip finishes, and as soon as I put a drop of glue onto the freshly tied and trimmed knot, James cried out from his crib in the other room.

That would have to do for the time being. I placed my tools down on the bench, the fly in the box, turned the light off, and shut the door behind me.

I cooked dinner for James and I, then put a plate of leftovers in the fridge for when Sarah finished work. Outside, a storm picked up its pace – the deluge continuing, the sound of rain on the roof intensifying by rolling into thunder and flashes of lightning.

I got James off to sleep, and about five minutes later Sarah pulled up in the driveway. The storm was still raging outside so we opened the blinds at the front of the house, sat and watched the lighting crack across the dark violet sky as the rain battered down relentlessly.

From inside it was quite the spectacle, and it was certainly better than whatever trash was on television. We sat for at least an hour or two and discussed life, before eventually remembering our sleep deprivation and calling it a day.

Sleep came easy with the sound of rain on the roof, the light rumbling of thunder now in the distance, and the compounded months of sleep deprivation. My mind drifted to thoughts about the coming October long weekend and I hoped that, for once, it would be dry for the trout season opening.

CHAPTER 21 – THREE WEEKENDS, THREE SPECIES

Opening day came around soon enough and I was determined not to fight the crowds at some of the more popular spots. So I set my sights on the secret brook trout creek.

It was mid-afternoon by the time we reached the spot. The gravel road was fairly nice to drive on and there were no big plumes of dust following our car, which indicated that there had been plenty of rain up here on top of The Great Dividing Range.

We came down a slight hill and got our first glimpse of the creek – it was absolutely pumping with water! I'd never seen it up so high or running so fast, spilling over its banks and onto the surrounding grass in places. It made me nervous.

When I spotted another car and two men with fishing rods nearby, my heart sank even further. We parked and I had a quick chat with them. Thankfully they had just finished for the day and hadn't had much luck. We could take that one of two ways: one being that the conditions were bad and catching fish wasn't likely, or the other being that at least now the fish wouldn't be hook-shy if they hadn't been caught already today. My optimism chose the latter option! It had too, as there wasn't enough daylight left to drive to another creek.

We opened the car doors to a fresh and cool air. The grass through the scattered grey gums was intensely green. The sky was a vibrant blue, which seemed a foreign concept after the week of consistent rain. I grabbed my four-weight, Sarah's spin rod, then James' baby backpack. I hoisted James up into it, grabbed the rods, locked the car and we made our way downstream.

Before going as far as we normally go, I wanted to get Sarah her first brook trout, so we fished the lucky spot, right where the concrete pipes under the road spilled out into the creek below.

I handed Sarah her rod with a little brook trout patterned floating lure tied on.

A very short cast to the head of the pool, a few rotations of the reel and, just as I had hoped, a small brook trout hit the lure. It jumped a few times but had very limited hiding options due to the small bathtub-sized extents of the pool.

I bent down to net the fish and felt myself leaning way further forward due to James being strapped to my back. I quickly corrected for the extra weight, but had missed my net attempt. A few nervous moments passed before I got my next chance, and this time I got the fish in the net. At least I didn't drop James!

And it brought me such immense joy to help Sarah get her final New South Wales trout species ticked off, and to see her admire the uniqueness of the brook trout. A careful release and we made our way downstream.

We reached as far downstream as we were willing to walk, then turned around to fish our way back to the car. James was getting restless on my back, so Sarah attempted to bribe away his restlessness with a snack. He accepted the bribes willingly. Until he didn't.

Stopping by the largest pool in the creek, I took James off my back to let him stretch his legs. He stood on his wobbly toddler legs and made a beeline straight for the creek. We had to run after him to stop him going in. We corrected his course, and within seconds he was headed straight back to the water. It was now apparent that we would never be able to turn our backs for even a second with him out here at this age.

So we spent the next little while enjoying the afternoon and trying to play games and entertain him while one of us took turns casting into the bigger hole.

The fishing was very quiet and I was all but certain that no more fish would be caught for the day. Late afternoon was now upon us and the sun was glowing gold throughout the spindly gums. Getting James to go back into the baby carrier soon became a futile task and we decided to just walk him back to the car.

It was a very slow exercise, as he stopped to look at things, or attempted to make more repeated runs towards the creek. Making our way back at a snail's pace, I saw something I otherwise would have probably missed – a trout rose in the flooded grass section of the creek.

I had caught a rainbow trout in this creek before and assumed that was most likely what it was, as I typically hadn't seen rises before from any brookies, in my very limited experience. So I cut the dropper nymph off my line, applied some floatant to my elk hair caddis and began to cast it upstream. The fly landed just short of where I wanted it to, so I was lifting it to recast when I missed the first strike.

A quick false cast and I placed the fly back close to the fish's right-hand side, then watched its profile come towards me like a tiny origami boat on an ocean current.

The trout rose again to strike and missed. I repeated this exercise at least three or four more times. My patience was being tested and my resolve sharpened. I let out a little more line and this time landed the fly right up as close to the head of the pool as I could get, watching it slowly come back, closer and closer. The water around the fly moved in a flash of white water and colour below. I paused, then lifted the rod.

It was unmistakable this time, that feeling of tension, pressure, and most likely fear of the unknown from the trout's end. It was all in my hands, a tangible thing as I played the soft fly line back through my hands, a miniature tug of war where only one of us knew the end game.

I called for a net and landed my biggest brook trout to date. Not big by any real-world standards, but certainly big for this creek in northern NSW. I knelt down for a quick photo with Sarah and James before we carefully released the fish back into the water, which was now shimmering gold in the late afternoon sun. Just fifty metres from the car, it was the perfect crescendo to a great opening day.

CHAPTER 21 – THREE WEEKENDS, THREE SPECIES

The following weekend saw us steer clear of the busy Ebor opening pressure and head straight for our local rainbow trout stream. We had plans to be on the water before lunch time, but James and life had other plans.

Life was changing. What was once a simple get ready and go trip to the local, now required the planning skills of a project manager – working around feed times, nap times and organising extra gear and snacks. It was a different world, though of course one I would never change. We left the blacktop by mid-afternoon and cut our way up the valley following the road that mirrored the serpentine creek below.

Between the gaps of casuarinas, we could see the creek was up and flowing hard and clear. James was starting to crack it in his baby seat, the length of the trip just passing the boundary of what he was comfortable with at this age. Thankfully a few gravel bends later, we found our trusty car park by the creek vacant. James calmed down, and as soon as we had him unclipped he began to once again run excitedly to the creek. Boys certainly have a way of keeping you focused and busy at all times in the interest of their preservation!

I lifted him into his carrier so he couldn't run into the creek while I put my waders on and rigged the rods for Sarah and I. I rigged Sarah's rod first and she went to have a cast in her old faithful spot while I finished pulling the fly line up through the guides of my four-weight.

James protested his captivity and I assured him it wouldn't be long.

Soon enough, I slung him onto my back, grabbed my rod and began to walk down to the easiest spot to cross the creek. Given the height of the water and the precious cargo on my back, I sat on the edge of the grassy bank and shuffled my way down until my wading boots got a firm grip on the freestones below. Only then did I attempt to stand and make my way across.

With each step I found myself planting my forward foot, scuffing a little until it gripped before bringing the rear foot forward and repeating the process. The water was about mid-thigh on me in the deepest part of the creek. I looked upstream and the creek was stunning at this height. I unclipped the fly, let some line gently lay on the surface of the creek and cast upstream.

The flies in tandem landed in the strong current, my eyes fixed on the dry as they hurtled back towards me. The dry went under and I struck. In response, I was rewarded with a strong-willed and acrobatic rainbow trout, her enthusiasm surpassing trout double her size.

With the landing net in my left hand, I guided her in for a closer look.

She was pretty, a typical patterned fish from the creek we had grown to love. I held her up in the net for James to inspect and he seemingly garbled out his praise. Whether it was for the beauty of the fish or the skill of his father will remain a mystery.

After her release, I chanced my luck and made the exact same cast, only to catch another small hen rainbow almost identical to the first.

I repeated this again and felt immense gratitude for the health the creek was in after all the rain.

I had been standing mid-stream for a little while now and could feel James growing restless, so I made my way across the creek so I could let him out to toddle around while Sarah focused on fishing.

She was busy working the head of the first run, casting a lure beside a large rock that was usually exposed but was now partially submerged and creating a whirling vortex of water around it. We had caught so many fish close to this rock it was all but a guarantee. I watched expectantly, and when after a few casts she hadn't even had a bite I got a little concerned.

"Cast a few metres up past the rock into the really white water!" I called out over the low thundering rumble of the creek.

She didn't look back or give any sign that she had heard, but I saw the lure 'plop' into a mess of white water right where I had imagined.

I watched the green braided line dance above the rumbling creek with the steady rhythm of the spinning reel, and right about where it passed the rock the rhythm stopped and the line dropped into the current below.

With James in hand we walked up with the net and helped Mum land her fish. As was usually the case when fishing with

Sarah, it was to be the biggest of the day and, boy, did she let me know it!

I felt like we had only been here for mere minutes, but time had gotten away from us, just like the water rumbling down the valley.

Both having caught some fish and James having attempted to plummet into the creek more than once, we called it a day and waded our way back to the car.

That week at work, I had an idea. We had already been out fishing for the past two weekends and had caught both brook and rainbow trout... what if we backed it up with a third weekend warrior mission and tried for the trifecta with a brown trout. The premise of repeating that original single-day New England trifecta of my youth with a one-year-old was delusional at best. But three weekends and three species of trout? I thought that was a goal worth trying to hit.

I called Sarah on my lunch break and floated the idea out there for her to consider before the weekend.

By Friday afternoon, she too was on board with the idea. The hardest part was deciding just which of the creeks to try and fish, as most of my go-to brown trout creeks were hard to access, even without a small child attached to my back.

CHAPTER 21 – THREE WEEKENDS, THREE SPECIES

Then I remembered a grassy stream that my friend Jack had mentioned, where he had often caught some large brown trout. It was fairly pressured but was easy to access, kid-friendly (well, as far as bodies of water can be to a toddler), so it was worth a shot.

The car trip came with its usual dramas of a restless James and sleep-deprived parents. We pulled off the Waterfall Way at an unnamed rest stop between Armidale and Ebor to stretch legs, feed and change James. Once he was all smiles and giggles again, we climbed back in the car and pushed on for the final half hour of the journey.

We had just passed the big T-intersection outside of Ebor when I sensed it was quiet in the back of the car – a glance over my shoulder revealed that James fast asleep. Sarah and I shared some worried glances, because if he woke up before he was ready he would become irritable.

Pulling up to the gate, I climbed out to open it and tried as best I could to gently shut the door. Sarah then drove through the gate and I quickly shut it behind us so none of the very strong-willed cattle could chance their escape. When I opened the door again, it was to tears. Just as we had feared, James had woken up from his nap too quickly after I shut the door.

Thankfully with some kind words and reassurance that we had arrived, he calmed down as we drove down the last little stretch of track through the paddock down to the river.

It was mid-afternoon when we climbed out of the car, and with a little bit of distance between us and the water I unclipped James from his car seat, set him down on the grass to stretch his legs while we got geared up.

We went through what was almost ritual in nature after the past two weekends. I looked up as I pulled the chest waders up my body and saw James bring his hand up out of the ankle-high grass holding a rock the size of my fist.

He smiled. Not at me, but at the car behind me. Then he raised the rock up high.

I leaped forward with a speed that would rival the fastest birds and mammals – just in time to grab his wrist before he could finish firing his impromptu projectile at anyone's car.

Boys!

I turned him around and allowed him to throw it away from the cars, and with some hawk-like supervision I finished clipping up my waders. After I tied on a simple dropper combo of a bead head nymph and an elk hair caddis, we made our way down to the water. We were soon close to the headwaters of the river, where it started to become more serpentine in nature, weaving its way across the grassy paddock. The sun reflected gold and silver off of its scales of slow flowing water.

Once I was ready, I went to put James into the backpack, but he wasn't having a bar of it. We turned his energy to our advantage, getting him to walk slowly upstream alongside us.

We rounded a bend and I almost couldn't believe what I was seeing. A nice sized brown trout was simply sitting above a shallow spot in the river close to the opposite bank.

CHAPTER 21 – THREE WEEKENDS, THREE SPECIES

I knelt down so as not to spook the fish, took James with me, and pointed Sarah in the direction of the fish. James was determined to get to Mum, so I reached into the backpack and pulled out a packet of flavoured crackers to hold his attention.

I had him fully distracted now, as Sarah began to make casts to the fish that almost appeared to be sunbaking. James began to munch down the savoury crackers whilst bending down and picking up small rocks, sticks, bits of bark and anything he could see. Then he would lift it up to inspect and show me while garbling something probably very profound in his mind. I smiled and nodded while glancing over to Sarah, who was still casting over and over to the same fish.

"I can't get it to even look at a lure, you may as well have a go," Sarah said as she walked over to James.

I crept to the stream edge and, with the fish still in the exact spot, I made a cast and watched the flies drift towards him. About two feet before the fly was above him, the drift stopped and I realised the nymph had gotten stuck on some weed in the shallow water. I tried as best as I could to unsnag it without spooking the fish and managed about to do just that, then cut the nymph off and cast the caddis back out on its own.

This time it drifted straight over him, so I let it drift the remainder of the pool, as I knew that sometimes these browns got a little cluey with constant angling pressure and would sometimes wait until the last moment to circle back and snap something up. That was not the case this time.

I made a few more casts and got the same result. Before going insane, I changed the fly to the small Parachute Adams that Wags had tied for me, then made that same cast I had made countless times now to this seemingly lock-jaw fish. Then I saw something change.

It was small and subtle, just a slightly faster flick of a pectoral fin on one side and a slight adjustment to his position in the water. But I knew I had his attention now.

The next cast landed perfectly and this time he gave his fins a little kick and came up under the fly, casting a scrutinising eye before letting the slow current push him back to his spot. We spent so long trying to get this fish, I decided just to stand up and see if it spooked. The fish didn't even move. I waved my arms, but he just sat proudly in his spot. I decided that he had evidently played this game before and lost, and now spent his days rightfully suspicious of anything food-related.

We fished a little further up and had no more luck, not even seeing a fish, neither rising or cruising. The afternoon had fled us and we made our way back to the car. We had just gotten to the final big pool of water in the river before the car, when the last glimpses of the sun dipped below the trees to the west. I had given up on the idea of catching a fish. I was exhausted and so was my passenger riding in the backpack.

Then I heard something behind me. Turning around, I saw ripples spreading out from a single point across the slowly flowing water. A few feet away from the epicentre, the water sprung to life

CHAPTER 21 – THREE WEEKENDS, THREE SPECIES

as a nice brown trout leapt out of the water to snag something. In the now fading light I could see a small black mayfly dun appear on the surface between the two hot spots. I imagined a trout coming up from below and inhaling it off the surface in a moment of reckless abandon, one I had been hoping the fish upstream would have given into earlier.

I didn't have to imagine anymore – the water opened up into a void and the white mouth of the brown trout swallowed up the helpless offering. I steadied my breathing and unclipped the fly from the rod. The fish was working close by, so I didn't need to cast far at all.

Even with James on my back I laid out one of the best fly presentation casts I've ever done. Perfection, or seeming perfection, is often rewarded. In this case I was rewarded within seconds. The little pink post of the Parachute Adams, sitting high and proud on the water, was pulled into the water below. I had to stop myself from reacting too quickly and ruining the only take I had received all day. I paused, did a quick three count, then struck.

I think I heard that I had hooked the fish before I knew for certain through the thrumming in the cork grip. The sound of the fly line lifting off the water sings at a different tune when connected to something, as opposed to lifting the fly straight out of the fish's mouth. It's a fuller, richer harmony between man, water, fish, and the sky above. The alternative is like a loose out-of-tune string on a guitar.

Sarah was still fishing the next pool upstream when she heard me call out and came to give me a hand with the net. She had become quite proficient on net duty and managed to scoop the fish up in the first attempt. I cannot say the same is true for a lot of my 'mates'.

Sometimes it's hard to tell at first glance if it's a good fish or not when it is first netted. What I have seen is that the smaller fish lay flat in the bottom of the net, while the bigger fish writhe head-down and tail-up. When I saw this particular trout's spotless brown tail waving out of the top of the net, I knew it was a good fish for this system. I saw more fish rising all around the pool, in a frenzy to catch the mayfly that lingered too long, and that made my decision to keep this one for dinner the following night easier.

The following night while preparing the fish by bundling up some fresh herbs from the garden in the gut cavity, tying it up with roasting twine, and coating it lightly in oil and salt before going into the oven, I realised that I had done it. It wasn't the single day trifecta I had achieved years prior – life beat to a different rhythm now, a slower more deliberate tempo, full of lows and highs – but it was at a speed that allowed us to enjoy everything we had: a son we loved, each other, and the ability to go outside and bring back something different and fresh for dinner.

Chapter 22 – The World Changed

It was 2017 and closing season was fast approaching, I don't even recall if I had chased trout at all since the previous October. I was sitting at my desk early on Saturday morning, deep in study for my upcoming end of semester exams for my surveying degree, and my mind began to wander. I was getting distracted and irate, which was never a sign that my studying was about to get any easier or improve in quality.

So I went and found Sarah and said I needed a break from study. James was asleep, having just gone down for his nap, so she suggested I go for a fish and take my brother-in-law Beau, he and Sarah's sister Bec only lived around the corner.

I gave Beau a call, quickly grabbed some gear from the garage and drove around to his place. Beau wasn't a super devoted angler like I was, but he had grown up fishing like me and knew how to catch fish. We were chatting about gear in his garage when he realised he had a fly rod he had bought to take on another trip that we had both been on, though he still hadn't caught anything with it. We both decided today was the day to try and break the rod in.

That was when I told him, "The best way to catch your first fish on a fly rod, is to leave your spin rod at home."

He did exactly that.

I always loved the sound of four humming wheels dropping off the sealed road and onto gravel. It's how I knew I was getting close to the creek we had called home for so many seasons. Going around each bend and feeling the loose gravel through the steering wheel made me feel like any tension I was feeling was blowing away in the wind with the dust behind us.

The creek itself sat deep in the valley and, because it was already mid-afternoon, part of the valley was already in a cool dark shadow. The air was cold and dry. The creek was flowing, but only just, and crystal clear!

Crossing the creek was easier than it had been when the river was up, so Beau managed to jump across the rocks without even getting his feet wet. No sooner had we crossed, though, when I found myself gazing absently upstream and saw a trout rise no more than a few metres away.

I gestured for Beau to get into position. He made a cast that landed a little heavy and I thought would surely spook the fish, but I was wrong. The fish swiped at his fly and turned back upstream.

He made a much better cast this time and the fish took multiple swipes at the fly. I was worried the fish was going to run out of water to chase the fly in on the drift, when it struck one last time as Beau set the hook. Beau had just achieved something I never

CHAPTER 22 – THE WORLD CHANGED

had and never would, and that is catch his first ever fish on a fly rod on dry fly.

Fly fishing actually seemed to come naturally to him, as he landed another three or so fish all on dry fly for the day. It was a much bigger struggle for me, but maybe that's the beauty of learning something in your thirties with a mentor rather than in your teenage years going in mostly blind.

Still, I was getting desperate to catch a fish now, so when we came to the pool with a big log jutting out mid-current, and Beau not having waders, I stepped up to the challenge. In amongst the twisted grey timber, with cold water flowing all around and pressing against my legs through the waders, I saw a trout rise, right on the other side of the log jam.

Hooking him would probably be easy, but it would be landing the fish that would be a challenge. Yet hook him I did. There were a lot of tense moments with the four-weight as I begged him not to run directly under the log across the creek, but rather come over it. Thankfully he came right over the top and I managed to net him easily.

With my eye twitch now gone and stress levels back to some sort of baseline, we called it a day and headed home. It must have done the trick as I passed my exams the following week. Little did I know that the trout I had caught would be the last for a few years to come.

New South Wales received the lowest rainfall on record in over a century from January 2017 through to December 2019. From time to time, I would drive past some trout streams for work and noticed the water level dropping, the flows slowing, then stopping and drying up completely. The lush green was replaced by shades of harsh dry, dusty browns and reds. In the past, I had always looked at creeks and rivers as I drove over them, forever pondering what might be hiding in them. But now they were dry, the mystery long evaporated.

I no longer looked.

The icing on the cake of destruction came in the form of the 2019-2020 black summer bushfires. People died, homes were destroyed, as were countless animals. Smoke from the fires spread as far as South America and Antarctica. One significant bushfire ripped right through the Ebor area, completely decimating lookout platforms at the falls and connecting walkways. Another struck closer to home and razed my local trout stream, as well as a nearby pine plantation where we had fished and foraged for mushrooms for years.

During 2018, we had bought our first home, and in 2019 it was berated by dust storms coming off the barren fields outside of town. At the time we had evaporative air con, so all the windows

CHAPTER 22 – THE WORLD CHANGED

were cracked when the first one hit and filled our house with red brown dust.

Work was also hard going, hammering survey pegs into ground as hard as a bulls forehead in sweltering smoke laden hot dry air. I even spent one lunch break in a farmers paddock trying to dig a cow out of the mud where it had gotten trapped while searching for water in a dried-up dam.

If anything, it at least made it easier for me to study on weekends, as there was no chance of going fishing. I even let my fishing license expire. It was far too depressing to think about what was being destroyed. After the state had been on fire for the majority of the year, everyone was praying for rain.

Glimmers of hope can show up anywhere, and one Saturday morning I was cooking bacon and eggs and cracked a double yoker! Not long after that I dreamt I saw two young girls, playing carefree in a lush field, red hair flowing wild. It was a very vivid dream and I told Sarah about it, and almost twelve months to the day of my double yoker, we welcomed twin girls with red hair into the family in September 2019. They gave me such hope for the future, and that things would get better.

Sometimes you truly understand the meaning behind the old clichés 'be careful what you wish for' and 'when it rains it pours'. For that was in January 2020 when it started to rain. I guess no one dared ask it to stop after it had not rained for the past few years. So it just kept raining. The now full rivers broke their dusty brown banks and swept up everything around them. With little to no vegetation left to protect it, the dirt below didn't even put up a fight. So the rain led to flash flooding and started a few landslides, along with closing roads, destroying bridges and reshaping rivers completely.

In amongst all the smoke, drought, flames, dust, heat, and eventually flooding, rumours also came through the news about a respiratory virus in China.

I knew the trout streams would take years to heal from the damage of the drought, but little did we know that we would soon be forced to stay at home anyway. The cataclysm of events of the past few years now burnt onto the landscape and into our psyche.

The rivers would never be the same, and neither would we.

The world had changed.

Chapter 23 – Embers

In amongst the chaos of the new Covid-19 world, I resigned from my job. In between looking for jobs and faced with the prospect of sitting still for months or more, I got the courage to start selling homemade spice rubs under the brand name 'Hohnke Outdoors'. It was received far better than I imagined and I sold out of the entire first batch in the first few days!

But as well as it was going, I still had bills to pay and a university degree to finish, so when I got offered a great job with a civil construction company as a surveyor, I accepted. Soon enough I was back into the swing of full-time work, making batches of spices on weekends, and Sarah taking the reins to make sure the website orders got sent out while I was at work.

It wasn't long before I had to go to the small village of Guyra, its main claim-to-fame being Australia's highest elevation caravan park, and a festival dedicated to lamb and potatoes, two of the region's biggest industries. While there, I messaged my friend Luke, who had done some work in the area previously; and he gave me some directions to a creek and access point out of the village, a little bit of a drive but not too bad. He also assured me it would be free from bush doofers, unlike the stream where I had sent him to years before.

At this point, I hadn't fished in a while and I didn't really feel like it, but with the prospect of either sitting in a motel room after work, or going fishing, the choice was simple. I went back as quickly as I could to the motel to get changed, then unpacked my trusty four-weight rod from my duffle bag and got back in the ute. It wasn't long before I left the bitumen behind for glorious gravel, dust flying up behind me and glowing in the golden hour light.

I found the recommended spot and got to work setting up my rod with a trusty dry / nymph setup, locked the car and stumbled down through some rocks to the creek. The access was just under a low-level timber bridge and this was where Luke had said he'd caught some fish.

No sooner had I emerged from the long grass and rocks, below a canopy of gently whispering casuarinas, than the unmistakable sound of a trout surface feeding broke the tension of the water. A sound I hadn't heard in years. I looked around, took in the landscape, and realised this creek was very similar to my favourite creek back home.

Something deep inside of me kindled in that moment – an ember covered in ashes blown back to life. Each time that little trout greedily took something off the surface, I felt more and more kindling being thrown onto that ember. I hadn't felt like that in years. I had perhaps come to think that my love for fly fishing had died along with all those trout in my home creek in the drought.

But that wasn't it; that wasn't it at all.

Turns out, I had subconsciously disassociated my love for it to protect me from the heartbreak that had come with that drought. I guess that's just how the human mind survives – we rationalise what we feel to try and justify and avoid feeling our heart break. Like jaded lovers who suddenly claim to hate each other after years, often they don't hate each other at all, they just have a quarrel over something or other. Sometimes it's over something big, sometimes it's over something small, or a thousand unsaid small things. But rather than working through the pain to reconcile that love to what it was, they believe it's easier to say they hate the other. It's the mind's dirty trick to keep our heart safe.

However, the heart can't be lied to forever. It's only a matter of time before that hidden ember is exposed and breathed back into life.

So in that moment, I came back to myself. As I breathed in aromas of freshwater and earth, the water sang the songs of the creek as it cascaded under the bridge and over the freestones below, and that trout rose again. My muscle memory kicked in. I placed a dab of floatant on the dry, a Royal Humpy and made a cast to the last known spot.

The trout swiped greedily and missed the dry. I recast and this time the dry went under and I struck – she had obviously not been fussy and had preferred the nymph. She would have been around twenty centimetres or so, and in fighting fit condition, but nowhere near the right size to take for dinner.

After that it got quiet. I fished the same hole with no luck before moving downstream. It was a good hour before anything happened. The sun was just beginning to set when the seemingly barren hole I was now in stirred to life. Trout started rising everywhere!

I cast to where a few were and watched as they rose around my fly without ever attempting to touch it. I had to be decisive, I cut my two fly rig off and went searching in my fly box as I squinted in the fading light to catch a glimpse of what they were eating. I'm no entomologist, and I don't pretend to be – I had no idea what the small bugs were, but my best guess for an imitation was a size sixteen blue dun.

A dab of floatant around the hackles, a very short cast no more than three metres in front, and a greedy trout took my uneducated offering shamelessly. She was a mirror-image of the first fish, and I suspect they had been stocked into this creek on the same day from the same batch.

I caught three more in the twilight, as mosquitoes drank my blood and the stars began to reveal themselves to the sound of frogs and nocturnal insects. It was time to head back, even though the trout were still rising.

The person I was ten years ago would have stayed and fished into the dark, but I guess I had gotten better at being grateful and savouring what I had. I no longer had the desire to always be seeking more and was quite content walking away from still rising fish.

As I drove back into town, the car headlights revealed a small stand of radiata pine trees. I drove past them and thought about how cool it would be if there were pine mushrooms under them, though being summer it was almost impossible. Then again, being 1300m above sea level there are always surprises. I knew curiosity would keep me up that night if I didn't look, so I did a U-turn turn, went back and parked next to the trees. Climbing out in the dark, I turned the light on my phone and began circling the first of the big trees. These were very old pines, at least double the diameter of the biggest ever found in a plantation. And, sure enough, as I rounded the first tree I found a small clump of weeping boletes 'suilius granulatus'.

These were a staple find of ours back home, and I was especially fond of dehydrating them and grinding them into a powder to unlock their rich almost nutty fragrance. Not far from those, I also found my first slippery jacks 'Suilius luteus'. I hadn't found these around Nundle yet, but had been assured they were there.

Moving to the next tree, I found a half-chewed weeping bolete with a very unapologetic slug about four inches long with almost tiger-like stripes sitting atop his prey. I let them be. I filled my hat with my findings, brushed some pine needles and spiderwebs out of my hair and face, then jumped back in the car.

Back at the motel, I transferred the mushrooms from hat to lunchbox and turned in for the night.

I didn't come back to the area for a few months, and when I did it was peak winter and right in the middle of closed season. The cold up in that area was something else and I found myself working faster than normal in a vain attempt to keep warm against the sleeting rain, just so I could get back to the site office to process the data I had been collecting.

My cheeks stung with the cold under the hood of my rain jacket. I pulled the hood cords tighter but it was futile. I pressed 'store' on the data collector of the rover for the final check shot, then made a beeline back to the site sheds.

The survey data processed while I tried to warm back up, as the little wall-mounted rattler heater / aircon struggled in the conditions.

Everything done and saved, I folded up my laptop and jumped in the ute. I had something planned, and though I thought lots about not doing it on the drive back, I kept telling myself that the trout loved the cold – so I made the turn and started heading out of Armidale towards Dumaresq Dam, which is a year-round fishery like Sheba Dams.

I'd only tentatively dropped a line in here once before, and I figured with a bit more experience and local knowledge it was worth revisiting.

CHAPTER 23 – EMBERS

It was still windy and lightly raining when I arrived, but given I'd already been out in it all day I knew another half an hour before it got dark wasn't going to kill me. Well, not immediately anyway.

I tied on a favourite wet fly, a Tom Jones in a size eight to my four-weight, and walked all of five metres from where I'd parked to the water. There wasn't another soul around on the gently sloping granite sand banks, nor was there anyone enjoying a picnic under one of the large radiata pines. No children frolicked on the monkey bars of the playground. It was just me and my arrogant belief that, even in this wretched weather, I could catch a fish with only half an hour of light, and next to zero experience with the fishery.

It felt good to send some tight loops out over the wavy surface of the lake, and watch the wind push the entire line sideways like I was fishing a large river rather than a body of still water. I entered into that deeply rhythmic almost meditative state that comes from repetitively blind casting wet flies on still water, so I guess about fifteen minutes had passed when I felt a slight tension on the line.

I pulled into it and the line immediately left my cold numb finger and began to peel off against the direction of the wind. The line cut through the waves and I knew I'd hooked a good fish.

I couldn't believe my dumb luck, but maybe dumb luck favours those who are dumb enough to fish in weather like that. A few nervous minutes later, and without a landing net, I beached the fish on an incoming wave and picked it up by the tail. Something between a shout of joy and laughter left my mouth, complete and utter disbelief mixed with sheer joy and elation painted plainly on my wind-kissed cheeks.

She was a decent-sized fish somewhere above three pounds at a guess. It was most certainly a personal best fish for the four-weight.

Clearly a broodstock hatchery fish with a chopped tail, and I made the decision to take her home for dinner. I utilised the whole of this fish – she was full of roe and, not wanting to be wasteful, I found a recipe online and began to process it to have some poor man's caviar. It was quite an involved process separating out all the eggs by gently rubbing them over a metal grill, and I found – as my hands were under the cold water of the kitchen tap – that it felt warm compared to the freezing lake. The whole process was worth the effort, and each time I ate some of the smoked trout or had some of the roe I relived that catch again and again.

Chapter 24 – Rebuilding What Was Lost

I have always been amazed at where the rivers of fate have deposited me over the years and, in 2022, I had an opportunity to work by the very river where this story began: near the Guy Fawkes River.

A surveyor is usually the first person on site – establishing control, placing bench marks and setting out the proposed works. This particular job was no different. I placed my survey marks and began to traverse through the worksite, at the same time savouring every moment of combining what I did for work with being in a place I loved – a place that had been such a huge part of my life so far.

It was also a spectacular spring day: a pure blue sky with a UV index clearly off the charts, as I already felt its bite on my skin. There was next to no wind, with the exclusion of a welcome gentle breeze – the kind of weather you dream about on open season weekend when it's pouring with rain and the wind is blowing it sideways into your face.

But God and the weather rarely favours the weekend warriors and opening weekend aficionados, preferring to reject their part-time love for the outdoors and instead favouring the unemployed and the retired. Mostly because the trout bum often devotes their life to chasing trout because they love it more than anything else, and because the retired will have weathered enough storms in life, work, and those typical wet weekends to be shown some grace.

That day I fitted somewhere in the middle, stumbling into the blessed mid-week weather, fearing it may flee at any minute.

But it stayed, so as soon as I finished packing up after 5pm, it was time to rig up and fish upstream. I decided to stick fairly close to the pub and fished the beat upstream from the bridge. The fishing was quiet, for a long time I didn't even see so much as a lazy rise, and put it down to open weekend pressure still affecting the fish weeks later.

The grass along the river's edge was lush and green and as thick as I'd ever seen, coming to the top of my work boots. The river level was solid, not too high, not too low. By rights, the fish should have been fired up.

I worked my way up around the first bend and that's when life started to emerge from under the water. A small trout started feeding midstream about ten paces in front, and after a few unsuccessful offerings she took a well-placed cast that I allowed to drift back past her, which in her cunning she circled back to intercept.

She was only small and I recalled a conversation with the old man in Launceston who had first taught me to cast a fly rod, and him telling me about the Guy Fawkes. I can still see him in his

CHAPTER 24 – REBUILDING WHAT WAS LOST

sage green vest with tools and fly boxes at the ready holding up his thumb and index finger about four inches apart and saying, "All that way for one titbit."

I laughed a little inside and released the fish back to the river, sharing his mutual amusement. I wondered where he was now, and wished my mind wasn't like a sieve when it came to names.

No sooner had I released her than another trout rose in the same spot. She was a much nicer-sized fish, taking the fly greedily. I kept this one.

Then, as the sun dipped down below the escarpment to the west, the river boiled with life. Without even moving, I saw a fish skimming the surface and feeding in a small back eddy on the left-hand side of the stream. A section of bank had washed away and created a small pocket about the size of a car tyre and it had a slow swirling current separate to the rest of the river.

Getting a cast and presentation in front of this fish was going to be a challenge. The trout had obviously had an education in false offerings, and regarded my first dozen casts with complete disdain when the current gripped my line and ripped it from the area with unnatural speed.

In a rare moment of genius, I recalled some casting drills I had learnt from my fly casting instructor Peter Morse a few years prior, one that involved casting straight in front. But while the loop was going forward, you're supposed to move the tip of the rod from side to side so that the fly went straight, but with the line landing in a shape not unlike a Christmas Tree.

"What would I ever use a cast like this for?" I had asked very sceptically, suspecting this was purely a showmanship cast.

"Believe it or not, Ben," he told me, :the wiggle cast can be used when fishing a still pocket of water surrounded by faster moving water – the zig zagging loops get pulled away first, leaving the fly in the strike zone for as long as possible."

Night was falling and I didn't want to make another dozen futile casts, so I chanced on Peter's fancy cast. I was off the mark on the first one, but I executed the second one almost perfectly. The fly landed true and hovered in the head of that small back eddy of slowing swirling nutrient-rich water, just long enough…

The trout shed its scepticism, first a twitch of a fin, then in turning to face the fly. The cast was going to work! She broke the surface of the water in an instant and took the fly. I counted to three in my head and struck

I felt the hook find its place and she began to rage across the water. She had been careful and cautious but the cleverly placed fly was too good to be true. I found some good footing in amongst the tall grass, finding a spot where my feet wouldn't plunge through the marshy grass and into the water, then lulled her into the net just as daylight breathed its last. Shining stars began to pierce the indigo sky, dancing effortlessly on the riffles below.

I walked back to the ute, the slimy cork grip of a fly rod in my right hand, and a fish hung by the gills on the index and middle fingers of my left hand. The air was crisp and cold now night had begun, the bite of the spring sun a faded memory. I took a deep breath and filled my lungs with the pure air, and as I exhaled I said a quiet prayer of thanks. I facetimed the kids to show them the fish and said we would cook them up once I got home.

Though I was alone in the dark, my heart was full. I had a family at home that loved me, the work I was doing was meaningful, and I'd like to say that my hobby was bringing me joy.

Not that I believe 'hobby' is the right word. It sounds cheap, something you buy a few bits of gear for and off you go. Fly fishing is more than endless bits of gear. It's an all-consuming extension of the self. It allows us to observe creation and also to be creators, as we tie bits of feather and fur onto carefully selected hooks in our best attempts to recreate creation.

Sometimes we catch fish and simply observe, marvel at their designs and let them go. Other times we decide to take the fish to create meals and to nourish our bodies with wild food from some of the cleanest rivers on the planet. The older I get now, the more I tend to care about how I cook those meals, and whether it does justice to the life that was taken to provide it.

As for these particular trout, I carefully reverse-butterflied and removed all their pin bones. One I then gave a light dusting of Salt Bay seasoning and put it in the smoker with some banksia pods I had foraged on the road side on my way home. The banksia pods have a beautiful sweet fragrance when put into a smoker, not too strong and very versatile – Australia's best kept BBQ secret!

The other fish I placed skin side-down on the charcoal grill with nothing but some olive oil and salt on the skin. I placed a small pan as a weight across the top to keep the skin even on the grill.

The kids made short work of the smoked fish with their fingers, which brought to mind my eating those first few trout straight out of the smoker by the river up at Ebor all those years ago. I thought of Jason, Mark and Tim, and knew we were all raising families of our own now.

I took the other off the grill and gave it a few generous pinches of banksia-smoked finishing salt I had made a few weeks prior. It was the best fish I had ever eaten. The crispy, lightly salted skin allowed the true flavours of the fish to come through. Sarah and I sat at the kitchen table and we finished the last of it together while we watched the three kids run around in the backyard.

A part of me realised then that my younger self would have felt like I needed to be out on the water again, to not be 'wasting' time at home and good weather windows. I didn't have those thoughts anymore, I simply felt content. I had worked to provide, I had caught some fish, and now I had brought them home and shared them with my family. Tomorrow we would go to church and catch up with family, before repeating the week again.

Fly fishing no longer had an urgency to it, like I needed to be out doing it as often as possible. It had simply become a part of life, a life that now truly felt full as I worked those deeper, slower pools and left the fast shallow riffles.

Chapter 25 – Snow Flake Caddis

I needed to be in the Ebor area for work for a few weeks to make sure construction got off to a good start. It was during these few weeks that I began to take advantage of the few hours of light left thanks to daylight savings and go back through and revisit some of those creeks I had fished with Jason all those years ago.

This was a convenient task, as I was staying at a house on the edge of Dorrigo, and these little adventures simply formed part of my afternoon commute.

One afternoon, I came around the big sweeping bend in the road that had once been veiled in mystery and fog, and was now marvellously exposed in the golden afternoon light. I found the angler access point and headed downstream as I hadn't been down there much before. Cattle let out some moos from across the fence and ran alongside me with a look that was either cautious or curious about whether I was carrying some tasty treat that I wasn't giving them.

Their paddock came to an end, and I lost my ten-strong beast shadow as I approached the water. Something inside me told me to slowly peer over the edge of the bank into the large pool about twenty feet below. I crouched down beside a tree and I slowly peeked around it.

Below was a pool about the size of a tennis court, no doubt the largest on the creek. The water was slightly discoloured and moving slowly everywhere except the main flow on the far bank.

Directly below me was a brief movement, and realised it was a brown trout foraging the edges of the pool, not far out from some overhanging shrubs. I slowly climbed down the bank, being careful not to silhouette myself against the sun on top of the bank and throw a shadow over the fish. When I dared not get closer, lest I sent some loose rocks scuttling down on top of the fish, I pulled out some line and tried to guess just how much I needed to reach the fish and avoid getting hung up in the trees below.

Casting was way more difficult than I had imagined with the steep angle of the bank, it was almost like I was punching down. Still, I did my best and prayed that the fly would land gently and not like a punch thrown into the water.

I landed the fly gently enough given the circumstances, about six feet in front of the fish on his all-familiar beat. I thought he hadn't paid it any attention, and I might have to recast. When he was about a foot away and I was almost certain he would fin his way straight past, he changed course slightly.

After a flash of white he opened his mouth and, without even making a noise or a splash, he took the fly.

CHAPTER 25 – SNOW FLAKE CADDIS

I paused momentarily before striking, but when I struck the fly came straight out of his mouth and hurtled back towards me! A light spray of water came off the fishless line. The brown disappeared and never resurfaced for the rest of the afternoon.

So began an afternoon of seeing a few more browns, usually as they were torpedoing upstream and away from me, but it was nice to know they were still there.

The stream headed west for a section and the water was ablaze with golden light, and soon within that light began to appear some snow flake caddis. Not many at first, just a half dozen or so flickering around in the glow. It was enough to get the browns looking up.

Then the number of them began to surge considerably – tiny graceful white wings fluttering against the radiance of the sun, darting around whimsically in the soft breeze as they flirted with certain death lurking in the water below.

One began to push the boundaries between this realm and the next, but even the boundary isn't a safe place when a brown trout is on the other side. Sure enough, the underworld opened and swallowed the hapless victim without mercy in a spray of glorious water.

As one aquatic predator after another launched their attacks from below, so then did a land predator cast other attacks from above.. No malice, no ill will, no aggression, no noise. Just a man balancing the scales by laying out an elaborate array of line, then a tiny piece of sharp metal clothed in dubbing, thread, feather and hair that sat on the boundary between the two realms.

The tables turned and the aquatic predator thought he had yet again bested his prey, while unknowingly taking in a trojan horse. He realised his folly all too late in the gift that was all too good to be true. He rained down his fury between his realm and the next in a spectacular show of scales and water. To a caddis he would have looked like a true dragon. A beast weaving through the sky, gleaming scales, beauty and terror, and a gaping maw with an insatiable appetite for their kind.

The caddis rose higher to avoid the commotion, but needlessly. In his fury, he unlodged the fly and left both of us defeated. The true victor of the day were the caddis as they waved their tiny white flags and retreated into the trees.

In the dying light of day, I had to again walk back to the car alone.

This was the first stream in NSW where I had seen so many snow flake caddis. I had seen some around Miena in Tasmania, though nothing like the tales I'd heard of Tasmania's mighty Shannon Rise, and how so many caddis emerged at once. Tomorrow I would try another creek.

I couldn't help but think that the access at this spot had become more overgrown. Small spikey shrubs and razor grass curtained down the abutments of the small concrete bridge, in a display that was visually striking with various green and gold shades. While pleasant to the eyes it certainly wasn't pleasant to be walking through, I amassed a collection of cuts and pin pricks across my legs and arms while searching for that second creek. I couldn't ever remember this area being so overgrown. At times I had to battle my way through the shrubs by getting down on my knees and threading my fly rod through seemingly impossible gaps.

While crawling under a fallen tree, I found a strange brown shape with a symmetrical spiral pattern sitting on the moss-covered rock now beneath me. A type of snail about the size of a fifty cent piece. I have never seen another like it.

Still I continued crawling through shrubs, under logs, and down embankments holding onto forest vines. Each step released the damp fresh earth from the forest floor, while in the background I could hear the falls below. Not deafening like the main falls in town, but much gentler, and with very different scenery.

I made it as far downstream as I dared to fish back from, knowing that nightfall was inevitable, and found a spot where the vegetation opened just enough to permit me to stand on its edge about one third of the way up the pool. Vines hung from gums, ferns and shrubs filled the floor. The water was dark with a hue of grey, the stream bed sodden with sediment beneath the steep earth and moss banks. Jams of fallen trees and branches created a variety of fish habitat and prevented me from being able to cast to the fish as well as I would like.

Still, a small brown trout began to rise. We had only ever caught browns in this stream, but it was so overgrown here that I could only manage a small roll cast downstream in the direction of the rising fish from my clump of earth.

It landed short. Considerably short. I fed the line down the guides and let it drift down slowly. The fly bobbed and swung over the surface of the water. The current grabbed a hold of the belly of the line and the fly went hurtling downstream at an unnatural pace for the water it was in.

I recast and had the same result. I didn't like leaving fish just to find more fish, but the afternoon was getting on. Down here in this deep part of the gully it was already too dark to wear my polarised glasses. I took them off and placed my usual glasses on before moving to the head of the pool.

I had to clamber down and around a large root ball of a fallen gum tree. But as I peered around the next bend in the creek, I saw a trout rise over the shallow brown freestones, and snow flake caddis beginning to appear around the edges of the stream.

I kept my profile as low as possible and made a cast. The trout had a few missed swipes at the small caddis fly I had on, displacing water in the ankle-deep run. As I lifted the fly out of the water at the end of the run, I caught a glimpse of movement. A pale silhouette was gliding effortlessly with the ebbs and flows, barely seven feet away.

My quarry was hiding in plain sight. I made sure my hands were concealed behind the root ball of the gum, then made a short cast and landed the fly about four feet upstream of the trout. My caddis fly drifted back towards me while the caddis above danced with life, tormenting the trout below.

He must have thought his luck had turned a page, as he finned across the shallow freestones, lifted his head, opened his jaw and took the fly.

But it was not his luck that had changed but mine! Now, having won the battle of the minds, I lifted into the fish, and with a taut line began the physical battle.

He put up a great fight and did not come to the net easily, a true warrior fighting to the end. But with the fish now in hopeless surrender, I turned inward and battled with my soul. Should I keep the fish, or should I release the fish? My thoughts waged against one another, and with careful thought I gently removed the hook and slid him back into the cold water, then watched as he faded into the current. When I felt no sense of regret with my decision, I knew I had won the war. I hoped our paths would cross again.

When I came to the base of a waterfall, it was quiet. Not a single trout disturbed the surface of the large opaque pool. I cast a few times and the fly drifted lazily back to me in the slow-moving water. I decided to try for something different, tied on a streamer and began to work it through the pool. The line came up tight, too tight, and I knew I had set the hook on a large submerged log.

Unable to free it, I admitted defeat and sacrificed the fly, reeled up my line and began to clamber back up through the ferns and vines while there was still light left in the grey sky.

Out of breath from scaling the sharp incline to the top of the falls, I took a moment to look back and admire the water cascading over the edge. Silver light gleamed through the overcast sky in the west, through the gentle sway of the towering gums. The caddis danced safely above the water, snowflakes that would never become snow.

Thunder rumbled in the east as I drove out of the site office compound the following afternoon. Fishing the streams around Dorrigo was out of the question for that day, but I could certainly chase some trout if I was quick and chose somewhere close. So I stopped the vehicle opposite the pub in the main street of Ebor. Rigged up and ready to go, a single caddis fly tied on the end of my leader, I changed out of my hi-vis orange work shirt and into a dull fishing shirt.

After then walking down the bank to the river through the lush grass, I caught movement against the green grass hanging over the opposite bank. There in the shadow of the bank, against the flowing water, was a swarm of snowflake caddis, all hovering about half a foot above the water. The wall of them was easily twenty feet long, sweeping around the river's gentle curve. Although individually quite uninteresting, in this swarm they moved in a rhythmic wave motion, each contributing to the whole ensemble, and what a delight it was to watch these small seemingly insignificant bugs put on a display that clearly had the hands of the divine upon it.

I don't believe the spot they had chosen was by mistake. It was over some faster flowing shallow water clear of where the bigger resident trout liked to hang out. A slightly stronger wind began to push from the east, likely feeding off or into the pending storm. As that wind touched down on the river, and turned the gloss of the river to a haze, the snow began to fall in reverse.

Now all around me and above the river was filled with the small pure-white bugs – a simple bug that has captured the attention of fly fishermen from all around the globe for over a century now. I began to wonder, there in the midst of the thousands of tiny white moths, if this is what those early fishers of the Shannon Rise had seen?

I'd never heard of anyone talking about snow flake caddis hatching around Ebor before, which is not to say that they weren't happening, but rather that it was not common knowledge in my fishing circles.

The sky above was now a mix of silvers, whites and swirling dark blue. With my eyes turned to the heavens, the caddis now appeared as a swarm of black and grey, like ash raining down against the bright clouds above.

A few years ago, this small town had experienced one of the worst wildfires known for the area, quite literally on its back steps; and, as I regarded this incredible flurry of snowflake caddis, I tried to imagine the flames engulfing the trees as the fire swept up the escarpment and crested the ridge, and the town itself under an ominous orange sky, thick with rancid smoke and raining down ash and embers. There on the edges of the escarpment, the blackened trunks of once towering gums stood testament to the horrors that had swept the land.

But such thoughts didn't last long, fading into the back of my mind as the vivid green grass, the cold flowing water, and the promise of afternoon rain came back into crystalline focus. Bright white snow flake caddis now completely filled the sky, like doves descending from the heavens, offering hope for a better future as fresh foliage sprouted all around from the blackened landscape. The season of destruction had passed and a rebirthing was now in full swing. Nature was healing and here was I, working in this magnificent place to help rebuild the manmade.

Every event in my life – where I had worked, what I had studied – had led to me being there on that seemingly random weekday afternoon, to witness the greatest caddis hatch I had ever witnessed.

I had seen a huge mayfly hatch at Little Pine Lagoon on Tasmania's central plateau. My friend Tim and I had been having the most horrendous week of fishing, and late on our final afternoon in the highlands the gale force wind had finally subsided on the untouchables shore. Under a greyed-out sky, knee-deep in the frigid water, wader boots half stuck in silty mud, small black shapes had begun to appear on the silver surface. In the eerie calm, those shapes had transformed into miniature sail boats as they unfurled their mainsails and sailed north east along the wind lanes. The great leviathan then arose from the dark water and swallowed them whole on mass. I managed to trick one of the great beasts to take my offering in amongst the thousands of mayfly duns littering the surface of the lagoon, and I remember him fighting wildly, leaping out of the water numerous times, his great bronze flank marked with striking black circles. I almost had him to hand when the line slackened, and on closer inspection he had straightened the hook of my fly. There was power in names, for I realised they didn't call it *The Untouchables* shore for nothing.

But even that great hatch at such a world-famous fishery paled in comparison to what I was witnessing now in the New England of New South Wales. The caddis rose and fell as they laid their eggs on the surface of the water. The cycle of life in its natural rhythm. Creation: life, death, and birth fulfilled in front of me.

What followed would also be the best session I'd had in my life to this point. Around the next bend, the trout were rising with purposefulness and single-minded focus, it was hard to distinguish rises from ripples as the surface of the river forgot what it was in the commotion.

My first two casts left me with two fat rainbows in the forty-centimetre range, weighing about a kilogram, both from the same spot. They could have been twins! I kept these to take home and share with the family. I then caught a handful of other fish, some smaller, some the same size, though released them all.

The snowstorm of caddis continued on and the trout kept feeding, into the evening twilight and beyond.

A younger me would have fished into the night. But I had learnt that sometimes the best thing is to quit while you are ahead, with steam left in the tank, and to take a moment to feel the joy afforded by the fishing, before fatigue sets in. So with the light disappearing, I stumbled homewards across uneven marshy grass with a brace of nice fish in hand and work to do tomorrow, occasionally watching the caddis continue to dance in front of the skylit sky.

I wondered if they would still be there the next day.

For the rest of that week I fished in the same spot, although the numbers of caddis seemed to diminish each day. There was still a regular afternoon hatch that resulted in, dare I say it, careless trout that were almost too easy to catch. I even fished the same pools and caught fish that looked the same as the day before, even though I had taken a few for the table. The river was beyond healthy, the trout were fat and full of life, the insects were breeding like mad, the green grass and foliage were spreading their tendrils, reclaiming the once blackened landscape. Life was good.

On my final afternoon of this marvellous hatch, I wandered to the end of the public access in town. I came to a fence across the river where a large black piece of conveyor belt was placed half in the water to stop animals, both bovine and human, from going further up or down the stream.

I assessed the seemingly forbidden section of river, upstream of the black rubber belt with rusty barbed wire over the top. As I expected, there were trout rising like mad there, almost like they knew they couldn't be targeted by the hack angler without a private access. But I figured I needn't break the rules, as I could stand and cast upstream by leaning over the fence, with only the barb wire getting caught in my shirt.

I hooked a solid little rainbow, though it managed to throw the hook. The rising fish seemed to move well out of casting range after that. I don't know how a trout has such profound spatial awareness to understand the length of a fly line, or even how that distance related to the fence, but they did.

I started to see some trout rising in the pool at my feet, so I made a cast and hooked a decent fish that buried me in the weeds and dislodged the fly. I don't know why, but I stayed at that pool for a while, staring at where the water flowed under the black rubber mat before rolling upwards. Bits of white foam were clinging to the mat at the edges of the main current. That's when I saw it, amongst the upward swirling current – a trout would occasionally roll up from the dark water and take a caddis stuck in the water rolling at the back of the mat.

All of this was happening mere metres from me. So I did the laziest thing I could think of and began to 'teabag' my caddis fly where the fish had last appeared.

He rolled back up from under the mat, went straight for the fly and inhaled it! I set the hook, then realised this fish was fighting with particular strength, a strength that genuinely surprised me. There were a few tense moments as he ran back toward the black rubber mat, but I quickly plunged my landing net into the cold dark water, amongst a gap in the tall grass, and led the fish in head first.

As I pulled the net out of the water, and saw the trout that was curling right up the sides of the net, I realised I had underestimated its size. He was a big bull of a rainbow, with a stunning pink strip running down his flank, flushed pink cheeks, and dark spots covering his olive upper half. Perfect proportions, and with a big powerful tail fin that wasn't clipped. When targeting river trout in the New England, he would be the goal of any angler – not a fish for the record books, but one that would remain etched into one's mind forever, a worthy adversary.

I walked back to the ute, set up my gas cooker, and fried some sausages and onions from the esky in a ceramic flameware pan on the park bench. It got dark quickly, so I finished cooking with the light of my headlamp, with bugs and hot drops of fat assaulting me from every direction.

Still, eating in the dark was atmospheric, with the sound of a storm approaching and a warm steady wind heavy with petrichor, surrounded by frog calls, and the rare passing car the only other sound. Alone with my thoughts, I began to realise how much this river had changed every time I had fished it over the past thirteen years. Always showing me a different side, or different appearance. Its fluctuating water levels, clarity, insect hatches, trout, banks, depths, riverside vegetation and seasons.

Reflecting on how much my life had changed in such a small window of time, I realised I had changed simultaneously. I had gone from a jobless adolescent trying to find his place in the world – exploring whether to be a musician, a vocalist in a metalcore band, a bookshop employee, a metal fabricator, a CNC machinist, a survey chainman and draftsman, a university student, and a surveyor – but all those were merely tributaries that had flowed into the main channel of who I truly had become at my core. A husband and a father of three wonderful children.

The river and I would always change, a simple reality of life. We would forever change with the seasons of life. As fluid as we both were, there was a truth inside both of us that was as solid as rock. It would still be a river and I would still be a fisherman. Yet our paths would forever intertwine.

Chapter 26 – Life is Fine Even Without the Pines

I had always intended to finish a long list of projects once 'university was finished'. One such project was a small bushcraft knife I had roughed out of a rusted machete that an old friend had left in the tray of my ute. I had shaped it out with an angle grinder, being careful not to hit the gyprock walls of our rental with grinding sparks, then placed it in a toolbox drawer, went back to study and all but forgot about it.

When we bought our first home in 2018, I found myself with a large double garage in the back yard, complete with a wooden work bench along the whole rear wall. So I made a jig with an eye bolt that I could adjust up and down to change the angle of the bevel and mounted it on the bench.

Late one night, with all the kids asleep, I then found myself out in the shed. File in hand and my piece of rusted machete blade mounted to the bench with a clamp, I got to work. I fell into a rhythm, slowly but firmly pushing down on the forward stroke with the file, before lifting and restarting. Each forward motion slowly took pieces of metal dust off and reshaped the rusted object in front of me into a shiny flat surface on the now visible bevels.

CHAPTER 26 – LIFE IS FINE EVEN WITHOUT THE PINES

Each forward motion also slowly changed the old rusted tool into an edge with purpose. Somewhere around midnight, my hands black and red, a pile of metal shavings underfoot, I dusted myself off and held the very knife-like shape out in front of me to look down the angular bevels that now almost touched. I left it on the shelf, turned off the shed lights as I shut the door, and went back inside the house.

A few winters later, my brother-in-law Beau called to say he had bought a second-hand 'coke' forge. I told him I had just the thing to test it!

That night, once the kids were in bed, I made the long drive across town to Beau's house and went out to his back yard. His forge was an old 44-gallon drum, black coke sitting in the top, above the air vent that came from the hand-powered air pump.

We placed the knife blade in amongst the coke and Beau got to work on the pump. Air flowed up the connecting pipe and through the scattered coke as it began to glow red and cast its radiant heat against the cold winter air. A few minutes, later the knife was glowing red. I touched a magnet to the blade and, when it no longer stuck, I grabbed it with tongs and submerged it in a container of waiting peanut oil.

Flames licked greedily along the surface of the oil before dispersing into thick white smoke. When I removed it from the oil, I grabbed a file and ran it along the edge. The hardened file now skated across the blade surface without so much as making a scratch on it. We had achieved what we set out to do. I now had my very own forged bushcraft knife.

Back at home, I placed the knife into the oven to temper it, relaxing the grain structure of the steel so it could now be sharpened and retain an edge without being brittle.

I then spent the remainder of the week cutting, glueing and shaping some Queensland black walnut pieces into a handle. I quite liked working with timber. Its sweet smells were a world removed from those of the carbon steel while being worked. Yet it is this combination of crafting with highly processed minerals and perfectly created wood, the fusing of manmade and divine, that creates such useful tools.

I sealed off the handle scales with oil, and watched in wonder as the almost dull brown timber came alive as the oil seeped through each small part of its finely sanded shape. A strong thread of ebony complimented the chocolate brown against the copper pins.

After a good sharpen, it was cutting through cardboard, paper, and the hairs on my arms with ease. I couldn't wait to get out and forage some mushrooms and clean some trout with it.

Late in 2019, amongst all the destruction at the tail end of the worst drought I could recall, I read in the news that a large fire had been deliberately lit in the pine forests at Nundle and destroyed

CHAPTER 26 – LIFE IS FINE EVEN WITHOUT THE PINES

millions of dollars of the softwood plantation. This forest had become so hugely sentimental to myself and others. I had shot my first wild pig with my bow here, foraged my first pine mushrooms, and just generally considered it our home away from home.

At that point in time, I had begun to feel numb to the effects of the drought, everyone was just in survival mode. We had already suffered the loss of one of our best trout streams, we now risked losing a second. Once the drought had broken and we began to finally go back to our old haunts, I was never really prepared, though, for what we saw as we wound our way up the mountain.

Whenever I usually rounded the corner at the border of the forest, where the native bush met the foreign pines, I was always amazed by the bold contrasting colours between the two, standing testament to the bond between old and new.

But this was not to be, and my heart was not ready to be greeted by the actual destruction we saw. Where there had once been towering pines, were now only burnt stumps, vibrant red dirt marred with tracks from bulldozers and excavators. The most jarring thing was being able to see every little rolling hill between us and the horizon, with only small surviving pockets of pines. What had once remained shrouded within the mystery of the pines, was now laid bare for all to see. The irregular shape of a bald head once all hair was gone.

We drove around almost aimlessly, down a few of the forest tracks, tracks we had travelled for decades, now completely foreign in what was both familiar and alien. It was very quiet in the car, the only sounds were the slow rolling gravel under rubber tyres and unvoiced dismay.

The next bend in the road revealed some bigger sections of pines unscathed by the fire. We turned down a rarely used fire trail and pulled over when we came to a fallen pine tree across the track. I unbuckled the twins and with James they went straight into the pines to see if they could find some pine mushrooms in the mat of amber needles below.

"Farnoons!" Emma exclaimed as she held up a nice hand sized Saffron Milk Cap for us to inspect.

I brought the basket over, just as I heard the cries of "Mushrooms!" from Claire and James up ahead.

I had my work cut out for me, following the kids and chopping off the dirt part of stems with my knife before placing them neatly in the basket. Within half an hour, the basket was full to the point of overflowing.

We set up a table behind the car, and with a gas cooker began to cook an assortment of sausages, onions and the fresh foraged mushrooms. Not many things in life smell quite as good as rendering fat, caramelised onions and the fragrant smell of saffron milk caps intertwined with the fresh earthy scents of a pine forest. Kids are always more willing to eat food they had either gathered or cooked, and this was no exception – they all finished their meals.

The kids then explored the forest fringes while Sarah and I cleaned up the pans and packed up our improvised kitchen. Finding these mushrooms, after the fire had destroyed so much, gave me hope.

With the afternoon still relatively young, I suggested we go and see if any trout had survived the fires. I prayed and dared to hope as we clipped the kids back into the car.

It took a while to get my bearings and find the old trail down to the creek, but eventually we were descending to the valley floor. The sun was approaching the ridgeline above to the west, almost touching the tops of a stand of a dozen or so surviving pines. A barren wasteland between us and them.

Surprisingly the creek was now much more visible, the fire having cleared the thick knots of blackberries that once carpeted the valley floor, although a few had now started to send fresh runners out across the ground. Finding a place to park the car was also now much easier, with a wide area left from machines.

All five of us then walked downstream a hundred metres or so, and when I came to the old crossing I realised just how much had changed. Where I had once stood on stepping stones in ankle-deep water was now waist-deep and narrow. No one had crossed the creek here in a vehicle for quite some time.

Looks can be deceiving, of course, and this was no exception to that rule. Yes, the blackberries were gone and so were the big trees that often posed as casting hazards. But they had been replaced by fresh blackberry runners that formed tripwires in the straw-coloured grass, and an assortment of other fast growing shrubs had taken hold on the creek bed. With small children under foot, it was too hard to go downstream further, so I pulled some line out and made a short cast with a caddis fly downstream, and gently released more line down the guides to keep the fly drifting with the fast flowing riffles.

As I was looking into the glare of the sun, it was somewhat hard to spot the fly as it rose and fell above and below the riffles as if riding waves. It crested one and, when it failed to reappear up the next, I lifted my rod and was rewarded for my observation. A small fat rainbow fought hard on the other end.

Safely in the net, Claire and Emma quickly inspected my just-too-small catch with much pointing, touching and observation, before we released her back towards the setting sun. She had been in stunning condition, the fattest fish I had seen in this creek.

The next pool was much longer and slower flowing. About two thirds of the way up the pool, a small tributary was pouring into the creek. A single small shrub outstretched into the creek at the confluence, and off the edge of that a trout began to rise.

The banks were not forgiving and I could get no closer than the small patch of gravel river stones I currently stood upon. I made my final stand here, made a pile of line at my feet, and made one of the longest casts I've ever done with the four-weight.

The cast took every ounce of skill and luck I could muster, and the dry landed where I willed it.

It felt like time stood still as the small caddis fly drifted around in an eclipse of the currents on the otherwise still water. Then it was gone. I had assumed it was just another small undersized fish,

CHAPTER 26 – LIFE IS FINE EVEN WITHOUT THE PINES

like the ones I had previously caught here. But with the taut line thrumming down the guides and through the cork grip I knew something was different.

There were a few tense moments as she evaded the net on the shallow gravel, but ultimately the battle was won. She was a rainbow covered from head to tail in black freckles, her silver flanks graced with a perfect blush pink stripe. I have never tired of catching rainbows and suspect I never will. Each is a master artwork in the gallery of creation, and a tiny hook covered in fur and feather is the grandest admission ticket.

By this point, James and Sarah had wandered down to get some photos of the girls and I with our catch, and at their request we kept her to cook.

It was a great opportunity to teach James how to clean a fish. Taking the knife I had made, standing on the edge of the creek, I guided him through how to make the incision at the vent, then guiding the knife away from himself and up to the gills before disconnecting them. Then it was as simple as pulling out the guts and casting them into the grass for the birds, foxes, and ants.

How could I so easily take and kill such a beautiful creature, you might ask. The truth is that it is not easy, I have always been very particular about where and when I take fish. Gluttony and greed are sins. Whereas food procured by the work of labour, along with an awareness of what it once was, gives us time to reflect on what we have; to not over consume or wish for more than our share. Whether I take the fish from the stream or a tray from a shop, something has to die to sustain our life. The natural emotions we feel when taking our own food helps us to maintain what is often removed from the thought process at the store, which can perhaps more easily lead to over consumption.

Driving home that night, I thought about how close it had been a 'perfect day'. Maybe if I had gotten up earlier and managed to hunt a deer, pack out the meat, and then go foraging and fishing I could have had a trifecta-like day, similar to the one younger me had chasing browns, brookies and rainbows. I realised, though, that this line of thinking was flawed, a type of greed to shake more than I needed out of the day. More importantly, it was a type of greed that put more value on my own interests rather than on spending time with my children. So I pulled that weed of a thought out by the roots.

We had found an abundance of mushrooms, fed well, and had now taken a nice trout home for our next meal. But most importantly, every one of us had enjoyed the day. We had all woken up when we were ready and gotten ready together as a family, the kids had explored and found lunch for us all. Sarah and I had spent time together and watched our kids enjoy themselves; we had enjoyed ourselves. Finishing the day with some fly fishing, I realised, was an added bonus with some extra teaching opportunities for the kids.

Considering the despair I had fallen into upon seeing the fire's destruction, I really should have been grateful we had found any mushrooms or fish at all. Deep down I found that I was content,

CHAPTER 26 – LIFE IS FINE EVEN WITHOUT THE PINES

my heart was full. My children were happy, my wife was happy, and I found myself grinning ear to ear as I reflected on the day.

The death of those trees had opened up new opportunities to fish. Like the old broken machete blade from the forge, new life had come from the flames here too. Destruction may come, but new life is always possible. Seasons come and go and change through the years, and so do we.

Chapter 27 – One For James

It had been a few seasons since the bushfires when I developed a single-minded goal: to get James to catch his first trout. Which is why we soon found ourselves on the edges of the Sheba Dam with James making cast after cast with a small trout lure. The air was cold, as spring had not yet found the mountains. A stiff breeze roughed the surface of the water, turning the reflection of the ancient gum trees from a photo to an abstract oil painting. But I wasn't even casting a rod myself, it was all about getting James that first trout. Plus my hands were full with the twins, who had almost reached their limit for being outside in the cold.

Accordingly, Sarah took the girls to the car to get out of the wind, and I stood beside James as I saw the enthusiasm drop from his face. I wanted to keep trying, like a problem gambler who was sure his luck would change at any moment if he kept going. After fishing for a good couple of hours, though, we cut our losses and went home fishless.

Opening weekend soon rolled around and spring was still nowhere to be seen. Opening weekends usually mean rain, but I

CHAPTER 27 – ONE FOR JAMES

must have done something right as we were graced with a merely gloomy overcast day. So it was time to try again.

On the banks of our favourite local stream, for the first time since the fires and drought, and the first time with the twins as well, I waited until Sarah had waded to the opposite more-fishable bank, then began acting as a human ferry to cart each of the three kids across one at a time in a surfboard style carry under my arm.

The water was flowing, clear and cold. The banks ablaze in greenery where the flames had been a few years prior. It was good to be back here. I just hoped the fish were too!

At the very least, I had figured it would have been restocked in that first year after the drought broke, in which case the fish should be around plate-sized by now. But I couldn't raise any interest, and neither could James with his small spinner.

We tried all of the best spots, and everything in between. Not even a flash, boil, or bump. The girls were reaching their limit once more, so this time I took them to the car and left Sarah and James to fish. I really hoped they would find a trout, not just so James could get his first, but so I could know that our home creek was healing.

It was quite a while before James and Sarah came back across the creek and up to the car. Sarah had only managed to catch a single small fingerling sized trout, which to me meant that it had only just been restocked this closed season for the first time. It would be another year before it was worth fishing again.

I had thought that this would have been a bona fide way to ensure James caught his first trout, but it wasn't to be. The rivers, creeks and dams had all changed so much and nothing was certain anymore.

Between Christmas and New Years Eve, a time I used to spend with my brother and my friends chasing trout, I was now with my own family, as well as my sister in law Bec, her husband Beau, and my niece Zoey, who were staying for a few days around Dorrigo. Perhaps this was another good chance to get James a trout? The time of year was great and the creeks were fishing well this season.

But first, we all wanted to go to the beach. So we wound our way down to the east and out to Sawtell. Now here was a town I hadn't visited since I was about James' age myself. It looked very similar, although it was far busier than I could remember, and we spent a good half an hour just trying to find somewhere to park. Finally stepping out of the car, though, and looking at that tidal creek, with its clear water and sandy flats, dragged me under a wave of nostalgia.

My father, and grandfathers on both sides, were all fishermen, and I had spent so many weekends and holidays by the water with a rod in my hand or waiting patiently with one in a rod holder that I didn't know anything different. I had gone willingly, and

CHAPTER 27 – ONE FOR JAMES

sometimes not so willingly, but could clearly remember the fish that had changed it all for me, the one that had made me actually want to go fishing.

I had been about ten, and I had a crisp ten-dollar bill to take to the tackle shop, which was up the main street of Sawtell. I remember the shade of the large fig trees in the median providing much needed respite from the coastal heat, but I had only one destination on my mind. The night before, we had watched one of my Great Uncle Mick's fishing videos, where a man had caught barramundi on soft plastics. I'd never really seen anyone use them before, they more just accumulated dust in the side compartment of any store-bought tackle box. But the way he talked about them and how they work had me intrigued. Now I was determined to try it.

I found the little tackle store and pushed the aluminium framed glass door open.

"Can I help you with anything?" the shop keeper politely asked, the words muscle memory from his mouth.

"I'm looking for some soft plastics," I replied.

His gaze noted the blue ten-dollar note in my hand, then he guided me down to the clearance bin at the front. "What type of fish are you chasing?" he asked. "Anything in the creek?"

I answered honestly.

He paused momentarily before plunging his hand into the pile of various packets before presenting me with two different types –

a bloodworm-coloured packet of small grubs and another packet, coloured black and chartreuse.

I took both, then he showed me some jigheads. I bought a few in chartreuse with a small black dot for an eye.

"If you go down to the creek and fish these off the drop offs, I can almost guarantee you will catch a flathead."

My eyes beamed, and with not a cent of change I said my thanks and all but ran back to the caravan park where we were staying.

Tying the jighead straight to my braided line before sliding on one of the black and chartreuse soft plastics, I told Granny and Pa my plans and ran down to the creek.

I waded out on the golden sand, the tidal water a welcome relief against my skin. Side stepping a few stingrays camouflaged on the bottom, I came to a drop off, made a cast, and was quite underwhelmed by the distance. I felt like it only went out about two rod lengths. Still, I worked the lure exactly how I'd seen the guy do it in the video. Before I knew it, the retrieve was over.

I made another cast and this time I felt something, though I couldn't really see through the dark water below me. I thought it must have been a snag, so cast out again, and the same thing happened. This time, though, I saw a flathead following the soft plastic to the base of the drop off.

The next cast brought him undone as he inhaled the small soft plastic when I worked it slowly beside him.

It was like time stood still – the mouth transformed in an explosion of white and sand, erasing the small black shape from

CHAPTER 27 – ONE FOR JAMES

the water. The fight wasn't even really a fight, the fish was well undersized and soon in hand.

I marvelled at his sandy camouflage, and while I was, he flipped off the hook and swam back down into the deeper water.

I had caught lots of fish before but something about catching that one, on a lure of my own, had me hooked.

Before taking my own family to Sawtell, James had himself already caught fish. About a year before he had caught a small bream on some bread at Lake Macquarie. Then again, just a month prior, we had been at Belmont on Lake Macquarie on a Sunday night, and he had decided to try his luck again. We had just been to Mass at the Sacred Heart Cathedral and, taking advantage of the last of the afternoon light, had bought some takeaway fish and chips and had gone to watch the sunset over the lake.

After feeding ourselves and the gulls, the kids were keen to fish. So I took all the rods out of the car along with the rest of the gear, handed James his rod and he went off up ahead onto the hardwood jetty, walking out on the planks as a purple and amber sky came to life.

I was dawdling up the planks like a pack mule with the girls rods and a bucket, while somehow also having a finger spare for the girls small hands to grip as they stopped on each plank to inspect something in the water through the gaps. James was already at the end and he made a big cast with a dark red coloured soft plastic.

"I've got a fish!" James yelled out.

I glanced up to see his rod bent right over and thought that he'd just snagged something. I said as much in passing to Sarah as she raced past us to help him.

"He's not snagged, it's a fish!" Sarah confirmed.

I dropped the gear to one side of the busy jetty and raced up with a net.

It was a low tide and I had to lean right over to net the fish, but it was a very respectable flathead in the forty-plus centimetre range. It was the only fish we caught for the whole of that weekend, but I couldn't think of anyone more deserving of it than James. He still hadn't caught a trout, but some fish was better than no fish, and who knows where his own fishing journey would take him, if at all.

Beginnings are often seemingly invisible yet pivotal moments on our paths, which can change the course of our lives. Or rather those moments in our lives that show us who we are becoming, and who perhaps we were always called to be. To everyone else those moments may be just another day ending in 'y', but to us they are a nexus. Only time will tell what that will be for James, Claire and Emma.

While our children may come from us, it is not for us to decide what their purpose is in life. It's our job to raise them right, in a loving home, before releasing them to their own individual

CHAPTER 27 – ONE FOR JAMES

purpose. A selfish part of me will always want my kids to be my fishing buddies! But forcing them into it might clip their wings, such that they can't ever fly from the nest.

I often hear people say you should fish while you can before kids, or that having kids all but ruins your life. Nothing could be further from the truth. Having children has improved every single aspect of my life. My kids have taught me how to be selfless. To live for someone other than myself. To use my time better. To be patient. To be grateful. To love and be loved.

Having kids has in fact made me a better angler, by forcing me to fish spots closer to home, spots that get fished heavily with easy access and to still catch fish in them. My younger self would have always been in the car searching for the next creek when the fishing got quiet, or hiking far from the beaten path. With kids I was forced to try a new fly, a different cast, or cast one-handed with a toddler in the other arm until I found fish, or fishing those deeper slow-moving holes and leaving the shallow fast-flowing riffles for the younger anglers.

Given what I have seen from those bright young children already, I think it's entirely possible that they will turn out to be nothing like me. Sure they may look like Sarah and I and have similar characteristics, but they all have wildly different personalities and interests.

All these rivers I have fished have shifted and changed so much since my first visits, after all the fires, droughts, floods and seasons of abundance. Yet here we both are, forever changed and changing. Forged by fire and storms, a constant force on an inevitable journey. Forever shifting; forever constant. Conduits of water; conduits of life.

Our kids will be the same, hurtling downstream shaped by the courses of their lives. Maybe there will be trout in their rivers of passage, maybe there won't. A river flows where it needs to and so do our lives. The water will always flow downstream. Eventually all water leads back to the ocean, and I now find the river of my life has found its way back to the sea.

Sarah and I recently celebrated eleven years of marriage and went into Sydney, doing some shopping and eating some dumplings with the kids after catching the train in from the Central Coast. In an almost full circle we found ourselves in Saint Patrick's Church – not the one where we exchanged vows in Tamworth, but one in The Rocks in the heart of Sydney. A truly magnificent gothic sandstone church surrounded by towers of gleaming glass and concrete.

The priest spoke to us after mass and asked where we were from, "Tamworth" was of course our reply. His eyes widened, as he was also from Tamworth! St Patrick's had been the church where he was raised! He knew the priest who had married us. Although I'm still relatively young, I'm too old to believe in coincidence anymore. He invited us and the children up in front of the altar and gave us all a blessing. The world is so big, yet so small, and the rivers of fate had once again carried us where we were always going.

Heraclitus the Greek philosopher once said, "No man ever steps in the same river twice, for it's not the same river and he is not the same man."

Indeed this wasn't the same river, but the echoes of what once was and what will be are forever present.

Almost two years after our trip to Sawtell, I found myself far from Tamworth, working by the sea on the Central Coast with the family in tow. Claire had fallen asleep on the lounge but Emma wanted to go fishing, and James was keen to come as well. So I got all our gear ready to fish from our local wharf on Brisbane Water.

We were almost out the door when James asked, "Can I bring my skim board?"

I had to let him down. "Nah mate, it's high tide and I can't watch you off skim boarding while Emma is fishing."

His head dropped with sadness.

I felt awful, especially since he had more coordination at ten than I ever did. So I reminded him that there would be time for skim boarding when Mum and Claire weren't stuck at home, and we headed off.

Walking down to the wharf, the early spring sun had finally begun to appear after months of rain, with its glorious warmth now caressing our skin. I had a bait rod each for James and Emma and a fly rod for myself.

I started off by casting a pair of weed flies around the pylons searching for luderick, then turned to help Emma. But while trying to re-bait her line, I felt a take on the flies.

A solid battle then ensued on my four-weight and, after some close calls with oyster-coated pylons ready to shred the line in intercession for the fish, I led the dark fish into a waiting net. Emma was so excited and wanted to hold it and marvel at its gleaming dark scales and stripes, while James took some photos.

Then something happened that I wasn't expecting at all.

"Can I have a cast with your fly rod Dad?" James asked.

"Of course, buddy!"

He made a few casts, though it was then starting to get late and I needed to get ready for a nightshift, so we made our way home.

The next day I woke up after lunch to three kids begging me to take them fishing! Evidently James and Emma were keen to go again, and Claire had obviously felt like she'd missed out while she napped.

"Dad, can you bring two fly rods today?" James asked.

"Absolutely!" I replied sincerely.

CHAPTER 27 – ONE FOR JAMES

The air was warmer, the sun beaming down harder, and there wasn't a breath of wind. But that meant the water was glass as the tide slowly rolled in, and clear enough to see stingrays, jelly fish and small fish on the fringes of the mangroves.

I set James up with my four-weight and a small bread fly, then crumbed up some bread and threw it out into the water from the end of the wharf. James made an excellent short cast, landing his fly in amongst the slowly sinking crumbs.

Then it was battle stations for me as I ran between each of the kids. The girls' bait constantly needed replacing, as it was being stolen by all the small fish beneath our feet. Still, at least they were excited that something was biting, so worth the waste.

James himself made another cast and I saw the fly disappear beneath the water. He pulled on the line and played the small fish that was biting – too small to need a net. A cute little brown and spotty smooth toad fish.

He was excited, and the girls thought the fish cute and asked to pat it, before asking if we could keep him as a pet because he was "so cute".

I laughed briefly before I had to shatter their dreams and explain that we had no way to actually keep a saltwater fish as a pet. So the girls patted him and told him he was beautiful before gently releasing him. It might not have been a trout, but it was never truly about trout anyway – it was about being together, while allowing them to grow.

Indeed, as I watched the kids fish, I remembered the Venerable Archbishop Fulton J. Sheen words, when he said that "Every child is an arrow shot out of the bow of its mother, but its target is God. Children have come through mothers, but they do not belong to them."

Over time, I will indeed find myself walking alongside their rivers, offering guidance, correcting courses, even teaching them to swim. Sometimes I might see the gorge ahead of them getting steeper, and know I must teach them what I can while I can, before they go where their life's currents take them. A place I may not be able to follow. If trout streams have taught me anything, though, it's that you never know where those serpentine creeks may bend back towards each other.

I once had no idea where my own life was heading, or so it seemed. But the truth is I had always wanted to get married, have kids and go fishing. I don't know why that ever felt like it wasn't a high enough calling; but through the bends, rocks and waterfalls of life I have learnt that it is.

As G. K. Chesterton once wrote, "The most extraordinary thing in the world is an ordinary man and an ordinary woman and their ordinary children."

CHAPTER 27 – ONE FOR JAMES

So that afternoon on the wharf I was at peace. A flotilla of white yachts and cruisers drifted lazily in the mild sea breeze. A pelican slept atop a pylon. Gulls screeched over some chips on the boardwalk. A crow sat above the light, watching with intensity behind his pale blue eyes. And the sun was warm on our skin.

No matter where the passage of James, Claire or Emma's lives may lead. That single moment was enough for me. My children will always be enough, simply being their father and raising them alongside their mother, the woman I love, is more than I ever dreamed.

I can't wait to see who we all become next.

Acknowledgments

The list of people I would like to acknowledge and thank stretches from the peaks of the mountains to the bottom of the ocean. If you feel you should have been mentioned here, please let me know and I'll be sure to include you in any further prints.

I would like to thank my wife Sarah, for loving me when the only thing I had to my name was potential, a car that constantly broke down, a handful of fishing rods, and a compound bow.

My children, for slowing me down so that I could see the beauty of life in all its intricate details, details that are otherwise missed when constantly chasing what's around the next bend.

My parents and grandparents, for all your support, values, and raising me outside often, even when I sometimes didn't want to be outside.

My older brother Mark, for always being down for one of my crazy adventures, even in less than favourable conditions.

Bec and Beau, not just for being family, but for being great friends that occasionally get roped into a long weekend of rainy misadventures.

ACKNOWLEDGMENTS

Jason, Tim, and Nick, thanks for always being down to hunt, fish and get away from it all, especially during those adolescent years; and to your parents for housing us, feeding us and often taking us hours from home for extended periods of time.

Hamish Brooks and Adam Collings, for being generous with your time and advice in helping me navigate the waters of finishing a book.

Will, Dale, and Bec, for often taking me into your home, feeding me delicious American food, taking me to the gym, work, the mountains to hunt, and rivers and lakes to fish.

Jenny, for always asking me to house-sit for you, even though I'm sure that you were just offering me some independence, and that your house didn't really need to be looked after. Thanks for being a good friend, and for feeding me when times were tough.

Barry, for telling us about the crazy spot below the falls.

Youngy, for getting me onto the brookies (even though I'm sure the drought took them out), the constant sledging, and for being a good friend.

Josh, for showing Youngy where the brookies were, and for teaching me that the NSW fly fisher only 'needs' two flies, a Royal Wulff for trout and a Surf Candy for salmon.

Wags, Straighty, and Richard, for the company and the banter.

The Ebor Dutton Hatchery staff, and acclimatization societies across our state, for without you and your ongoing work there would be no trout to write about in the pages of this book.

Zena Shapter, for putting your hand up to edit the manuscript and give me feedback. You were the first person to read the full draft, and I am sincerely thankful for your edits, highlighting areas for improvement, and positive feedback.

Non nobis Domine non nobis sed nomini tuo da gloriam.

Not to us, O Lord, not to us, but to Your name give the glory.

References

1. https://www.nationalparks.nsw.gov.au/things-to-do/lookouts/ebor-falls – Accessed 29/09/2025

2. https://www.britannica.com/topic/Guy-Fawkes-Day – Accessed 29/09/2025

The Author - Ben Hohnke

www.ingramcontent.com/pod-product-compliance
Lightning Source LLC
Chambersburg PA
CBHW020523080526
44583CB00013B/713